IMAGES
of America

HUDSON'S
DETROIT'S LEGENDARY
DEPARTMENT STORE

Dedicated to the leadership, determination and foresight of all Hudsonians who have left us with an amazing legacy of memories.

BUSY HUDSONIANS. This image from the 1940s depicts a portion of the Telephone Order Board Department on the 17th Floor. (Davis Hillmer Collection, Courtesy of Detroit Historical Museum.)

IMAGES
of America

HUDSON'S
DETROIT'S LEGENDARY
DEPARTMENT STORE

Michael Hauser and Marianne Weldon

ARCADIA
PUBLISHING

Published by Arcadia Publishing
Charleston SC, Chicago IL, Portsmouth NH, San Francisco CA

Printed in the United States of America

Library of Congress Catalog Card Number: 2004111637

For all general information contact Arcadia Publishing at:
Telephone 843-853-2070
Fax 843-853-0044
E-mail sales@arcadiapublishing.com
For customer service and orders:
Toll-Free 1-888-313-2665

Visit us on the Internet at www.arcadiapublishing.com

CONTENTS

ACKNOWLEDGMENTS

We gratefully acknowledge the assistance and guidance of Martin Austin, Jill Grannan, Patience Nauta, and Cynthia Young at the Detroit Historical Museum. A special word of thanks to Tony Jahn of the Target Corporation Archives, Wanda Jazowski, and Susan Kelly of Marshall Field's, and Alyn Thomas of Manning Brothers Historical Collection.

MANNEQUINS IN MOTION. Window shoppers in the 1930s were astonished at the sight of live models during a Hudson's promotion for swimwear. (Davis Hillmer Collection, Courtesy of Detroit Historical Museum.)

6

INTRODUCTION

More than likely, no other building in southeast Michigan has evoked as many memories as the famed J.L. Hudson Company department store, on Woodward Avenue in downtown Detroit. Generations of families still exchange stories of their experiences within what was once the world's tallest department store, whether they were employees, guests, vendors, or visitors.

Hudson's prided itself on carrying 553,921 items from A to Z . . . from aspirin to zwieback and antimacassars to zippers! No other retailer could duplicate the complete assortments of merchandise offered in over 200 departments from 16,000 vendors representing 40 countries. The store had 51 elevators to whisk guests to any one of 17 floors devoted to merchandise and services. (The amount of floor space devoted to sales was equal to that of 1,200 average-sized homes!)

Sales associates at Hudson's could speak in 14 languages and offered personal touches such as free taxi rides home for guests taken ill while shopping. Any item, regardless of size or value, could be ordered by telephone and home delivered (for many years, free of charge) via Hudson's large fleet of trucks. The store defined "one-stop shopping" long before we had hypermarkets or malls.

Fashion was constantly in the spotlight at Hudson's. The store collaborated aggressively with leading designers and manufacturers in the world fashion capitals. Whether it was weekly style shows in the 13th Floor dining rooms or at the Statler Hotel, designer trunk shows, or back-to-school extravaganzas in the spacious 12th Floor Auditorium, Hudson's was without a doubt always ahead of the game.

Active interest in the welfare of greater Detroit and southeast Michigan dates back to 1881 when Joseph Lowthian Hudson opened his first store on the ground floor of the Detroit Opera House on Campus Martius. Mr. Hudson's business was inseparable from his career as a remarkable citizen. As chairman and organizer of Detroit's Associated Charities, he helped lay the groundwork for today's United Way Foundation. To hospitals, churches, and family service organizations, his generosity was instrumental. The former downtown YMCA was made possible through his generosity and his personal fundraising efforts.

In the life of Detroit and Michigan, Mr. Hudson provided leadership and support to such community icons as today's State Fairgrounds, the Municipal League, Detroit Institute of Arts, the Municipal Lighting Commission, and the Detroit Board of Commerce. He also provided support to prison reform efforts, and to numerous social and economic issues that confronted Michigan's citizens at the time.

Mr. Hudson raised the bar for community involvement for the business leaders to follow. His dedication to the betterment of the community was actively carried on by his four nephews and successors, the Webber brothers, who stepped into the store's leadership upon Mr. Hudson's death in 1912. Richard, Oscar, James, and Joseph Webber led Hudson's into its second phase of growth as a giant in the world of retail. Under their direction, Hudson's volume grew until its sales made it one of the world's largest department stores.

Following the death of James Webber Jr., the remaining Webber brothers asked Joseph L. Hudson Jr., grandnephew of the founder, to join the firm. Young Hudson began his retail career on the downtown store receiving dock in 1950. Eleven years later at the tender age of 29, he was named president, the youngest individual in retail history to achieve this title. Under "Joe Jr.," the store entered its third major phase of growth. In 1969, Hudson's merged with Dayton's of Minneapolis, thus creating the Dayton Hudson Corporation. This merger, with Hudson's leadership, fueled store expansion throughout Michigan and into Indiana and Ohio. (In 2000, the Dayton Hudson Corporation was renamed the Target Corporation.)

Joseph L. Hudson Jr. led the store through two decades of change. His proudest achievements include the diversification of store and management staff, providing promotions and opportunities that previously did not exist. He aggressively pumped new life into the downtown store with an emphasis on fashion leadership and special events.

Hudson's was more than just a store. Hudson's meant community. Besides an exciting shopping experience, to many Michiganders the store simply meant the Freedom Festival Fireworks or the Thanksgiving Day Parade, a visit with the REAL Santa and Santaland, or attending a special event in the 12th Floor Auditorium. These were all "our" events . . . collective memories and experiences unique to this community.

The following pages in this book will provide you with a small vestige of Hudson's amazing history. The legend is further enhanced with the exquisite photography of Davis Hillmer. Mr. Hillmer photographed the store from the late 1920s through the mid-1960s. Many of these images have not previously been available for public viewing. Thanks to a generous donation from Mr. Hillmer's family, the Detroit Historical Museum is proud to share these with readers.

One

A Block-Long Monolith

HUDSON'S IN THE EARLY 1940S. Few individuals saw this overview, unless they worked on an upper floor of a nearby building. One can see the various additions to this massive structure. The roofline with the Hudson's name painted on the left (Woodward) side is the 12th Floor Auditorium. (Davis Hillmer Collection, Courtesy of Detroit Historical Museum.)

"THE BIG STORE" AT FARMER AND GRATIOT. This red brick Chicago-style structure was built in 1891 and contained 190,000 square feet on eight floors. At the time, it was the second tallest structure in Detroit. Hudson's earlier locations were in the original Detroit Opera House on Campus Martius and on the west side of Woodward, just north of Michigan. Note the Detroit Public Library in the foreground. (Courtesy of Manning Brothers Historical Collection.)

Phone Main 5164.

Woodward, Gratiot and Farmer Entrances to The J. L. Hudson Co., Detroit, Mich.

1912 POSTCARD IMAGE OF THE TWO HUDSON'S BUILDINGS. The building on the left depicts the 1911 addition on Woodward Avenue. Many folks thought the move to Gratiot and Farmer in 1891 was too far "uptown" from the town hub at Woodward and Jefferson. Mr. Hudson, however, made the store so attractive and the values so enticing that crowds deluged the retailer. (Courtesy of Michael Hauser.)

HUDSON'S GAINS ANOTHER FOOTHOLD ON WOODWARD. In 1914, construction crews demolished an existing building and began erecting a 10-story addition to Hudson's several doors north of the 1911 Woodward/Gratiot building. (Courtesy of Manning Brothers Historical Collection.)

HUDSON'S ABLE TO "FILL IN THE GAP." In 1923, the store acquired the building that housed Himelhoch Brothers and Company Clothing. This was an eight-story structure that stood between Hudson's 1911 and 1914 Woodward Avenue buildings. (Courtesy of Manning Brothers Historical Collection.)

COMPLETION OF "HIMELHOCH ADDITION." This image from August of 1923 depicts construction crews nearing completion of yet another 10-story addition, the former home of Himelhoch's. The red brick, block-long edifice so familiar to Detroiters was now taking shape. Smith, Hinchman and Grylls, the architects for the Hudson Block, took great care in making sure the various additions were consistent. (Courtesy of Manning Brothers Historical Collection.)

REPLACEMENT FOR THE ORIGINAL FARMER STREET BUILDING. In 1924, the former "Big Red Store" that opened as Hudson's in 1891 was demolished and replaced with a 15-story structure at the corner of Farmer and Gratiot. (Courtesy of Manning Brothers Historical Collection.)

HUDSON'S ACQUIRES NEWCOMB'S FOR NORTHWARD EXPANSION. In 1927, Hudson's purchased nearby competitor Newcomb Endicott and Company, located at Woodward and Grand River Avenues. Newcomb was a full-line department store that catered to the carriage trade but had been struggling to retain its identity. This image depicts the demolition phase of the Newcomb structures with frontage on Woodward, Grand River, and Farmer Street. (Courtesy of Manning Brothers Historical Collection.)

THE GREATER HUDSON STORE EMERGES. This 1927 image shows the Woodward/Grand River 16-story addition on the site of the former Newcomb Endicott Company. This addition stretched to Farmer Street and included the landmark 25-story tower portion of the store. The fortunes of Hudson's were running parallel with the explosive growth of Detroit. (Courtesy of Manning Brothers Historical Collection.)

THE HUDSON MONOLITH TAKES SHAPE. This spectacular image from 1928 depicts the 25-story tower addition nearing completion, as well as a service portion of the store, located behind the 12th Floor Auditorium. Two additional floors to the north (Grand River) end of the building were also added. (Courtesy of Manning Brothers Historical Collection.)

THE GREATER HUDSON STORE AS SEEN FROM FARMER STREET. One could not appreciate the massiveness of the Hudson Building unless it was viewed from Farmer Street. (Courtesy of Manning Brothers Historical Collection.)

The New Greater Hudson Store

The J. L. Hudson Company of Detroit is recognized as one of America's outstanding great stores. Modern merchandising methods are conspicuous throughout its 15 selling floors. More than 40 smart specialty shops, luxuriously appointed, were developed in connection with the store's most recent expansion. The history of the growth of Hudson's is one of the romances of dynamic Detroit.

PROMOTING GROWTH. In 1928, to coincide with the formal opening of the new Woodward/Grand River addition, Hudson's distributed postcards to create awareness of its enormous selection and unique services. Note that the artist has taken some liberties with the final depiction of the tower. (Courtesy of Michael Hauser.)

BUSTLING ON WOODWARD. It is difficult for young folks today to imagine a lively Woodward Avenue lined with retail, shoppers, and streetcars. This 1935 image depicts that energy. The five-story structure at Woodward and Gratiot was the remaining parcel that Hudson's needed in order to occupy the entire block. (Courtesy of Manning Brothers Historical Collection.)

HUDSON'S: A SOLID BLOCK OF STRENGTH AND VITALITY. This 1950s image depicts the 1946 additions to the store. Hudson acquired the structure at Woodward and Gratiot, demolished it, and built a 12-story addition to fill in the block. Additionally, the 19th and 20th Floors were added to the Woodward/Grand River building. The 19th Floor contained the Advertising/Marketing/Public Relations staff and the 20th Floor housed the relocated Switchboard and Supply Department. (Davis Hillmer Collection, Courtesy of Detroit Historical Museum.)

ORNAMENTAL FAÇADE OF HUDSON'S FARMER STREET ENTRANCE. This 1951 image depicts many of the ornamental cast-iron elements featured on the canopy and the various window ledges. The brass doors and nameplates are also evident. One of Hudson's most revered employees is standing guard at this entrance. John Williams (known simply as "William" to thousands of shoppers, vendors, visitors, and employees) was the official Hudson doorman/greeter from 1914 to 1959. Mr. Williams was known throughout the community for his sense of humor, politeness, and amazing memory. (Store Façade Image from the Davis Hillmer Collection, Courtesy of Detroit Historical Museum. Inset John Williams Photo Courtesy of Target Corporation Archives.)

NEW PROMOTIONS ADDED TO STABILIZE DOWNTOWN HUDSON'S. In 1961, Hudson's added "Good Ole Summertime" to its roster of promotions, designed to stimulate traffic at the downtown store. This week-long event brought throngs of shoppers back downtown, who, by this time, were getting used to shopping closer to home at Hudson's Northland or Eastland. (Davis Hillmer Collection, Courtesy of Detroit Historical Museum.)

ONE OF THE LARGEST OTIS INSTALLATIONS IN HISTORY. Otis Elevator Company installed 59 passenger elevators, 17 freight elevators, and 48 escalators in the Greater Hudson Store! Each elevator on the average made a round trip in two and one-half to three minutes and traveled nearly nine miles a day, delivering 24,000 passengers an hour to their floor destinations. Escalators were first installed to connect the two selling basement floors. In 1940, escalators were installed in the Woodward/Grand River building between floors one and seven. In 1946, escalators were added between floors one and 12 in the Woodward/Gratiot building. (Davis Hillmer Collection, Courtesy of Detroit Historical Museum.)

ELEVATOR ETIQUETTE WAS IMPORTANT AT HUDSON'S. Each employee of this department was provided with an "elevator phraseology" booklet that described how to greet passengers, call out various floors, and provide directions. Hostesses wore beige suits in the summer and black suits in the winter. By the 1970s, red suits ruled. The first African-American hostesses were hired in the 1950s. Because of the times, African Americans were not allowed to sell, but could work in specific departments like Elevators/Escalators, which were considered coveted positions. Ironically, their salaries were higher than those of their Caucasian counterparts on the selling floor. (Immediate Right: Courtesy of Detroit Historical Museum. Far Right: Courtesy of Target Corporation Archives.)

ℋ

ELEVATOR
HOSTESS
MANUAL

ONE OF SEVERAL ELEVATOR PENTHOUSES. This room on the 20th Floor held several of the 535 motors necessary to run the many elevators in the vast Hudson complex. In the store's heyday, elevator mileage per car averaged 240,000 miles per year. There were almost 40 miles of cable in the system. When the Greater Hudson Store was completed in 1928, the building featured more elevators under one roof than in any other building in the world. (Davis Hillmer Collection, Courtesy of Detroit Historical Museum.)

The operator in charge of this car was selected because she is courteous, capable and dependable. She will be pleased to do anything she can to assist you.

ANOTHER SIGN OF THE TIMES. This signage from the 1940s is obviously quite sexist by today's standards. Hudson's policy at the time was for all "hostesses" to be female, and all "elevator starters" to be male. (Starters arrived earlier and inspected each car, starting the motor and turning on the light, prior to handing the car over to the "hostess." The starter would also direct traffic to the "next available car.") During the holiday season in the 1950s, this department employed 125 associates. (Courtesy of Michael Hauser.)

PNEUMATIC TUBE SYSTEM. The tube system enabled Hudson's to provide quick service on all sales. It took only a few seconds for a carrier to travel from any department to the central desk, where charges and cash transactions were authorized by a staff of eight. From command central in the Third Basement, the system (initially installed in 1916 and later expanded) traveled up to the 17th Floor. The system was operated by one 120-horsepower and one 60-horsepower blower, both in the Third Basement. These blowers provided the pressure to operate 170 tubes (which handled 1,500 carriers) throughout the store. (Courtesy of Target Corporation Archives.)

MECHANICAL BEHEMOTHS IN THE THIRD AND FOURTH BASEMENTS. Most employees had no idea of the amount of mechanical wonders it took to make the Hudson complex work. These two basements contained a powerful paper baler, a large incinerator, steam compressors, tanks for circulating water, refrigeration tanks/filters/pumps, transformers, and switching rooms. A staff of 275 employees was responsible for maintaining this essential equipment. (Davis Hillmer Collection, Courtesy of Detroit Historical Museum.)

MANY PANES OF INTRICATE ETCHED GLASS.
For those who looked beyond the exterior
of the main floor, passers by could marvel at
the many etched windows that graced the
Greater Hudson Store from the Mezzanine to
the Ninth Floor. The stylized "JLH" logo that
was etched into windows also appeared in
advertisements, signage, and shopping bags.
Just how many windows had to be cleaned
at Hudson's? Try 2,600! Several intact panels
were salvaged for the Detroit Historical
Museum. (Courtesy of Michael Hauser.)

ORNAMENTAL PLASTER. Artisans
in the 1920s blessed the Greater
Hudson Store with decorative
plaster throughout the facility. Most
memorable were detailed columns
and molding on the Main Floor and
Mezzanine. The detailed molding
at left was in the Mezzanine
Tea Room. A number of these
pieces were salvaged and restored
by Chuck Forbes and placed in
the State Bar on Woodward at
Elizabeth Street, adjacent to
the State Theatre. (Courtesy of
Michael Hauser.)

CA-35100 HANDLED UP TO 30,000 CALLS A DAY. By the late 1940s, it was apparent that Hudson's overburdened switchboard needed a massive upgrade and new quarters. Following five years of planning, a new system opened on the 20th Floor in 1953. Hudson's now housed the largest private switchboard in Michigan and the second largest in the United States. (Only the Pentagon's was larger!) The Switchboard Department employed 200 associates and featured 30 positions, staffed by 52 operators. (Courtesy of Target Corporation Archives.)

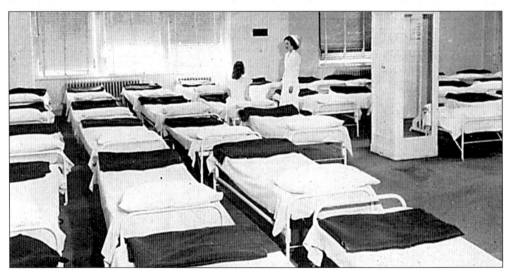

A COMPLETE INFIRMARY. From humble beginnings in 1910, by 1920 Hudson's Employee Hospital occupied 22 rooms on the 14th Floor of the Farmer Building and was staffed with four physicians and six trained visiting nurses. The staff assisted an average of 185 patients a day and could handle any emergency from a scratched finger to a broken hip. The main purpose of the store hospital was to take care of the minor accidents and ailments that arose from the 10,000 employees in the Greater Hudson Store. (Courtesy Target Corporation Archives.)

Two

THE HOLIDAYS!

HOLIDAY TRADITIONS. Everyone in southeastern Michigan knew that the "real" Santa was ensconced on the 12th Floor of Hudson's. Remember that thrilling express ride on the elevator up to Santaland? Whoosh . . . past 11 other floors magically filled with holiday décor. The 1949 image above depicts a three-story hand painted holiday sign on the Woodward marquee. This sign towered over a dozen live trees and the ever-popular "holiday castle."(Davis Hillmer Collection, Courtesy of Detroit Historical Museum.)

"IT'S CHRISTMAS TIME AT HUDSON'S." That was the store slogan for many years. It conveyed the magic and merriment of beloved traditions at 1206 Woodward. Legions of families would trek downtown from places near and far, initially by interurban trains and Department of Street Railways streetcars, and later by automobile. This 1941 image depicts a 60-by-80-foot holiday banner on the Woodward marquee. (Courtesy of Detroit Historical Museum.)

THANKSGIVING DAY PARADE. Hudson's extravaganza began in 1924 and initially consisted of three divisions, each led by a band with floats. A parade was not staged in 1941–1942 due to a shortage of materials at the beginning of World War II. Santa honored a tradition that began in 1924 and lasted until 1982 by climbing onto the Hudson marquee at the conclusion of the parade and receiving the key to the city. (Courtesy of Target Corporation Archives.)

TREE OF LIGHTS. Hudson's signature "tree of lights" debuted in 1955. It covered nine floors of the Woodward Building, was dressed with 5,000 bulbs, and required 50,000 watts of electricity. The tree was completely re-designed in 1964 to resemble a three-tiered tree featuring even more lights! The new tree was also nine stories high, 120 feet wide at the base, and took a crew of eight skilled workmen four weeks to install. (Courtesy of Central Business District Foundation Archives.)

DISPLAY WINDOWS ATTRACTED THOUSANDS DAILY. Occasionally window displays for non-fashion departments were allocated prime space for the throngs of pedestrians who passed by on Woodward, Gratiot, Grand River, and Farmer Streets. Many of these windows featured custom walnut walls, fringe draperies, and a small crystal light fixture in the ceiling. (Courtesy of Manning Brothers Historical Collection.)

NOT YOUR TRADITIONAL WINDOW DISPLAY. At Hudson's, the holidays were also an opportunity to promote departments and classifications that may not have received full attention in holiday newspaper advertising. An example is this 1933 image of a display devoted to men's wallets. (Davis Hillmer Collection, Courtesy of Detroit Historical Museum.)

HOLIDAY THEME WINDOWS. Another Hudson's tradition involved an entire bank of windows devoted to "Christmas in Many Lands," which depicted historic customs from North America as well as around the world. This was further carried out in the model home furnishings rooms on the Ninth Floor. Each room featured a hostess who was familiar with the language and customs of the country or region represented. (Davis Hillmer Collection, Courtesy of Detroit Historical Museum.)

DESTINATION TOYLAND! Before the advent of specialty retailers, Detroiters would not think of purchasing toys, games, puzzles, or dolls from anywhere but "Hudson's Toytown" on the 12th Floor. Just think of how many Red Ryders and Barbie Dolls were purchased from this virtual mecca for children, parents, and relatives! This image depicts a 1949 window display heralding the season opening of Toytown. (Davis Hillmer Collection, Courtesy of Detroit Historical Museum.)

FANTASY MECHANICAL WINDOWS. During the war years, window displays were less creative due to a shortage of materials. Displays at this time frequently supported the war effort. Interior and exterior holiday lights were dimmed. The 1950s saw a renewed spirit, propelled by a more robust economy and the initial suburban building boom. Thus the introduction of mechanical windows, such as the 1953 whimsical series depicted directly above. (Davis Hillmer Collection, Courtesy of Detroit Historical Museum.)

Opposite: **SLEIGH RIDE!** Holiday-themed window displays did not become crowd pleasers until the late 1930s. Display windows from the early 1930s offered browsers hope for more favorable times ahead. The window depicted top left, from 1949, is a simple holiday snow scene adapted from a Currier and Ives image. (Davis Hillmer Collection, Courtesy of Detroit Historical Museum.)

MECHANICAL WINDOW WONDERS. Hudson's legendary mechanical windows featured intricately designed themes that were planned well in advance, and in many cases took a year to construct. The bright colors and fanciful imagery they created captivated young and old alike. On weekends, crowds would line Woodward Avenue six deep to catch a glimpse of these creative wonders! (Davis Hillmer Collection, Courtesy of Detroit Historical Museum.)

TRADITIONAL MANGER SCENE. Regardless of the times, or of a particular year's "theme," Nativity scenes appeared in various forms through the years in Hudson's Woodward Avenue windows. Religious affiliations aside, show windows proved to be a wonderful escape from the ordinary. One was able to recapture distinct memories from simpler, uncomplicated childhood years. The above image dates from 1955. (Davis Hillmer Collection, Courtesy of Detroit Historical Museum.)

MAIN FLOOR HOLIDAY GARLANDS. This image depicts the Main Floor of the Farmer Street Building, facing Gratiot Avenue in 1940. The store decorated 28 large columns on the Main Floor with trees and garland. Ledges featured holly garlands with twinkle lights and red ribbons. Over 1,500 holly wreaths were placed around the rest of the store. Note the beautiful mahogany counters, detailed plaster, and the cast iron railings. (Davis Hillmer Collection, Courtesy of Detroit Historical Museum.)

DECKING THE HALLS. Hudson's holiday themes usually related to current fashion colors, playing off of two traditional colors, crimson red or hunter green. Interior displays were arranged for dramatic effect and their relationship to selling departments. Particular emphasis was given to the Main Floor of both the Woodward and Farmer Buildings. Most of the prep work for the holidays was completed in the 15th Floor Visual Merchandising Department. (Davis Hillmer Collection, Courtesy of Detroit Historical Museum.)

MODERN TIMES. The year 1946 saw Hudson's revert to a clean, stylized contemporary theme for the holidays as depicted here on the Main Floor of the Farmer Building. Each year the Woodward Building featured thick red carpet—six feet wide and 1,000 feet long—that lined the north/south center aisle. The chandeliers were adorned with garland and red lampshades, providing guests a warm holiday welcome from the blustery cold. (Davis Hillmer Collection, Courtesy of Detroit Historical Museum.)

A DISTINCTLY DIFFERENT THEME. In 1948, the store opted for an elegant holiday look. Gorgeous wall panels, commissioned exclusively for Hudson's, provided the illusion of depth to the entire Main Floor in both buildings. These unique nylon panels featured soft, muted colors and depicted scenes from Christmas legends and Biblical scenes. (Davis Hillmer Collection, Courtesy of Detroit Historical Museum.)

BILLOWING CLOUDS AND ANGELS. By 1953, the store returned to a more traditional holiday theme with billowing clouds atop the 28 columns on the Main Floor. "Legends of the Trees" conveyed holiday scenarios with "trees" of brilliance, birds, roses, goodies, music, and memories. They were complemented with large hanging stars and ornaments. (Davis Hillmer Collection, Courtesy of Detroit Historical Museum.)

STORYBOOK CHARACTERS. For the 1955 holiday season, Hudson's pulled out all the stops and featured an elaborate fairytale theme. Twelve vignettes above the Main Floor ledges featured larger-than-life scenes such as "Cinderella" in the image at right. (Davis Hillmer Collection, Courtesy of Detroit Historical Museum.)

AN ANGELIC HOLIDAY. The 1957 holiday theme featured angels high above the selling floor flanked by soaring arches and contemporary trees, adorned with many multi-colored glass bulbs and lights. (Davis Hillmer Collection, Courtesy of Detroit Historical Museum.)

FOR MEN WITH NO TIME, C. 1953. Another holiday convenience was the "For Men Only Shop." This hate-to-shop segment of our population was whisked up to the Seventh Floor via an express elevator. A single entrance, barred to women, opened into a walled-off area where "men only" could shop for their "significant others" in privacy. The only women allowed into this shop were secretaries, who were granted two hours of entry daily from 10:00 a.m. to 12:00 noon. (Davis Hillmer Collection, Courtesy of Detroit Historical Museum.)

GINGERBREAD TREE. The motif for 1956 modified the storybook character theme of the year before. Trees were adorned with candles, ribbons, and magnolia leaves. Fantasy tableaus included those from "Jack and the Beanstalk" and "Beauty and the Beast." (Davis Hillmer Collection, Courtesy of Detroit Historical Museum.)

HOLIDAY GREETINGS. For those who sought personalized cards, one could visit a gallery in a comfortable corner of the Ninth Floor. Guests would be seated at any one of 50 stations along several counters, as seen in this 1953 image. Books containing samples of holiday cards from more than 60 manufacturers could be examined. (Davis Hillmer Collection, Courtesy of Detroit Historical Museum.)

YULETIDE SHOP. Each holiday season, Hudson's 10th Floor became a wonderland of holiday trim and ornaments. The store featured Detroit's largest selection of imported ornaments from Germany and Poland. Note the display of Shiny Brite ornaments on the right. (Davis Hillmer Collection, Courtesy of Detroit Historical Museum.)

HOLIDAY BILLBOARDS. The store's signature slogan "It's Christmastime at Hudson's" originated in 1926 when it was coined by Mrs. Dorothy Bennet, a Hudson's employee. The renderings shown at left were proposals for the 1934 holiday season. (Courtesy of Detroit Historical Museum.)

A VERY SPECIAL HOLIDAY SHOP. The "For Children Only Shop" debuted in 1959 on the Fourth Floor, and was an immediate success with both children and parents. This shop was specially designed with display counter space lowered for children's easy accessibility. A staff of 35 trained associates assisted children as they began their shopping adventure. All items were priced to fit the limited budgets of young shoppers. Each child was interviewed with his or her parent or guardian prior to entering, and gift selection information was pinned to his or her coat. (Davis Hillmer Collection, Courtesy of Detroit Historical Museum.)

TOYTOWN EXTRAVAGANZA. Hudson's toy department was known to thousands simply as Toytown. This department would actually double in size during the holiday season, becoming the largest toy store in Michigan. Preparation for the holidays took three weeks, employing 25 carpenters and 13 painters, involving extensive scenery and fixture assemblage. The above image from the 1930s captures the Art Deco theme for that season. (Davis Hillmer Collection, Courtesy of Detroit Historical Museum.)

TOYTOWN AND SANTALAND. During the holidays, a common sight on the weekends would be the thousands of parents and children lining up to see Santa and visit Santaland. During the 1950s and 1960s, up to 450,000 guests would visit the 12th Floor, with lines occasionally stretching down to the 10th Floor. The glittering array of holiday toys and decorations gave grown-ups just as much pleasure as it did the little ones. (Davis Hillmer Collection, Courtesy of Detroit Historical Museum.)

CASHIERS' PARCEL DESK CASHIERS' PARCEL

Opposite, above: TOYTOWN'S ELEGANT LOOK IN 1940. This paradise for children portrayed a number of popular storybook characters on a faux stained glass background. Note the character toys from Disney's "Pinnochio" and the cartoon character "Little Lulu." A unique feature of Toytown was the Hudson Toy Advisory Bureau, which counseled parents and organizations on the selection of toys for children of a particular age group. This bureau was also in demand for speaking engagements before women's clubs and similar organizations. (Davis Hillmer Collection, Courtesy of Detroit Historical Museum.)

Opposite, below: HUDSON'S SANTALAND LEGACY. Through the years, the area on the 12th Floor adjacent to Toytown was known as "Santaland," "Fantasy Forest," "Twinkling Starland," and similar names. It covered one-half acre of floor space and consisted of a walk-through forest of snow-laden trees, thousands of lights, and enchanting animated figures. In the mid-1970s "Santa's Big Top" even included carnival rides, miniature horses, and a restaurant just for children. The image shown opposite left, below, shows Toytown in 1944. (Davis Hillmer Collection, Courtesy of Detroit Historical Museum.)

MEMORABLE MEMENTOS. In 1933, Ann Preston Hughes, a Hudson's employee, designed and wrote a holiday booklet that the store distributed to Santa's many admirers in Toytown. Each year, Ann devised a new theme. Left is "Patches" from 1937, and right is "Santa has a Circus" from 1938. (Courtesy of Michael Hauser.)

CHRISTMAS CAROL'S COLORING BOOK

CHRISTMAS CAROL'S COLORING BOOK. In the early 1960s, Hudson's own Christmas Carol found herself the subject of a coloring book, a delightful memento provided to each child who visited Santa. Christmas Carol also assisted Santa and his elves in the toy workshop. (Courtesy of Michael Hauser.)

A SATURDAY MORNING TRADITION. Another cherished Hudson tradition began in 1961 with "Breakfast in the Candy Cane Room." By then, two of the 13th Floor dining rooms had been combined to create the Riverview Room. The room was gaily decorated for the holidays. Entertainment included clowns, a magic show, holiday favors, and visits from Santa and Christmas Carol. The image above is from 1970. (Courtesy of Target Corporation Archives.)

A Well-known Holiday Visitor. The concept of "Christmas Carol" was born in 1950, when Hudson's was searching for a general assistant to Santa Claus. This cute young woman (Maureen Bailey) with shoe-button eyes escorted children to Santa's lap and assisted with distributing holiday remembrances of a child's visit to Santa, usually a coloring book or holiday story book. Christmas Carol also appeared with Santa in Hudson's Thanksgiving Day Parade. A staff of 30 helpers (Pixies, as they were affectionately called) assisted Christmas Carol. (Courtesy of Target Corporation Archives.)

KRIS KRINGLE IN 1947. Each holiday season, legions of families would trek to downtown Detroit from greater Michigan and Ontario to see the REAL Santa at Hudson's. Santa's first throne was installed in 1926. Back in those days, with Detroit's many immigrant families, Hudson's Santa spoke in five languages. In the late 1950s, Santa would host up to 20,000 visitors a day in his quarters on the 12th Floor. In the 1970s, Hudson's was the first major department store to feature an African-American Santa. (Courtesy of Target Corporation Archives.)

Three

Always a Fashion Leader . . . for Family and Home

Runway Show, 1947. The leading designers from the United States and Europe were prominently represented in Hudson's apparel and accessory departments for women, located on the Fifth, Sixth, and Seventh Floors. Over 400 fitting rooms were available to guests on these floors for suits, dresses, sportswear, furs, shoes, and millinery. (Davis Hillmer Collection, Courtesy of Detroit Historical Museum.)

THE FLOOR OF DRESSES AND COATS. The Sixth Floor of both the Woodward and Farmer Buildings was devoted to dresses and coats for women, misses, and juniors. It was an elaborate floor, furnished with American Walnut fixtures and paneling and soft, deep, pile carpeting. As viewed in the 1935 image above, the rectangular grid and open floor plan enabled maximum flexibility. (Courtesy of Manning Brothers Historical Collection.)

A MORE UPLIFTING FEEL. In 1936, Hudson's completely renovated the Sixth Floor. The result was a dynamic Art Moderne look that featured streamlined furnishings, column mirrors, wide-open areas for displays, and organized built-in display closets. Another plus for guests was the even illumination which flooded a great deal of the floor space with pleasant light. (Courtesy of Manning Brothers Historical Collection.)

AN ENTIRE BLOCK OF GENTEEL HOSPITALITY. This spectacular image depicts the depth of the renovated Sixth Floor in 1936. A guest was stimulated with beauty and relaxed in comfort. In today's economy, with emphasis on dollar sales per square foot, a floor set up like the one pictured above would be a tremendous drain on profit. (Courtesy of Manning Brothers Historical Collection.)

AN ELEGANT HOTEL-LIKE SETTING FOR THE SEVENTH FLOOR. In 1948, Hudson's gutted the entire Seventh Floor of the Woodward Building and introduced the Woodward Shops, which were designed to serve fashionable women who shopped with a discriminating eye. The block-long series of beautifully-decorated rooms included a shoe salon and shops known as the Town and Country Shop, the Green Room for better dresses, the Gown Salon, Fashion Coats, the Millinery Salon, Accessories, and Casual Clothing. (Courtesy of Manning Brothers Historical Collection.)

Motor City Chic. Where else but Detroit would fashions and automobiles collaborate? Each year, Hudson's displayed new models from every major auto manufacturer. Special dollies were inserted under each wheel, and then the auto was carefully steered into a freight elevator and taken to one of the three fashion floors. (Davis Hillmer Collection, Courtesy of Detroit Historical Museum.)

Further Streamlining in the 1940s. This 1944 image from the Sixth Floor further demonstrates the ongoing simplification of departments. The use of glass-block bricks created a boutique feel to segmented departments on the various fashion floors. (Davis Hillmer Collection, Courtesy of Detroit Historical Museum.)

MEN'S FURNISHINGS. In the 1920s and 1930s, merchandising principles were quite different than they are today. Most clothing items were displayed behind glass in large walnut cabinets. Rows of tables lined the aisles where guests could actually sit down and coordinate their purchases. Note the number of floor-length mirrors. (Davis Hillmer Collection, Courtesy of Detroit Historical Museum.)

MAIN FLOOR MEN'S. The Store for Men encompassed portions of the Main Floor, Mezzanine, and Second Floor of the Woodward building. This view is at Grand River looking south. In the 1920s, Hudson's began developing its own brand names such as Rackham, Aldrich, Kenmoor, and New Directions. (Davis Hillmer Collection, Courtesy of Detroit Historical Museum.)

MEN'S ACCESSORIES IN 1943. Furnishings that were located on the Grand River end of the Main Floor included shirts, neckwear, collars, scarves, gloves, dress jewelry, belts and buckles, handkerchiefs, hose, and other accessories for street and dress wear. (Davis Hillmer Collection, Courtesy of Detroit Historical Museum.)

RENOVATED SECOND FLOOR MEN'S, 1959. By the late 1950s, men's fashions required new presentation concepts, coordinated to provide guests with design, fabric, and color ideas. Shirts were no longer tucked away in drawers and suits were not behind glass. (Davis Hillmer Collection, Courtesy of Detroit Historical Museum.)

Interpreting The Metropolitan Influence

METROPOLITANISM in a man's clothes is something hard to define but easy to distinguish. You recognize it readily as well-poised, easy nonchalance —a sort of effortless elegance.

But, like all things of refinement, its subtle simplicity cannot be created without conscious effort and proper knowledge.

In Detroit, Hudson's Store for Men represents the metropolitan influence. When you buy your clothes here—your business suits, dress clothes, topcoats, hats, shoes and other accessories—you have the assurance that we have thought out your problems for you.

Experience, accurate knowledge of style, and ability to interpret the metropolitan influence with authority are integral factors in our service to men.

HUDSON'S
Store for Men

METROPOLITAN INFLUENCE AD. This sophisticated ad was part of a series that ran in selected publications like the *AAA News* and *Detroit Athletic Club News* in the late 1920s. The campaign was designed to solidify Hudson's fashion leadership with an unparalleled selection and commitment to service. (Courtesy of Michael Hauser.)

FOURTH FLOOR CHILDREN'S SHOPS. This floor was not only spacious . . . but pretty! It resembled a well-planned nursery. Specialty shops on this floor included the Baby's Own Shop, Juvenile Shop, Girl's Shop, Children's Shoes, Children's Furnishings, Children's French Room, and Candy Shop. In later years, Toys was moved to the Fourth Floor from the 12th Floor. Initially, this floor also housed the circus-themed Children's Barbershop. (Courtesy of Manning Brothers Historical Collection.)

SPORT AND SKI SHOP. The origin of this department dates back to 1928. With the growth of winter sports, Hudson's carried a full line of skis and ski apparel, and even sponsored ski clubs for young people. Additionally, this shop stocked all the necessary items for golf, camping, and fishing. (Davis Hillmer Collection, Courtesy of Detroit Historical Museum.)

CASBAH ON THE THIRD FLOOR. Everything a guest could possibly desire for fabric needs could be found on this floor. Here were woolens, silks, rayons, cottons, linings, laces, embroideries, patterns, and trimmings. Each week, 20 designs were made up from patterns in Hudson's workrooms, then exhibited and modeled for guests as part of the store's "Self Made Chic" program. (Davis Hillmer Collection, Courtesy of Detroit Historical Museum.)

AN ENTIRE FLOOR OF FURNITURE. The Ninth Floor Furniture Galleries, as shown in the above 1928 image, were paneled and fixtured in English Oak of the Tudor period. Guests could peruse home furnishings at all price levels. A highlight of this floor was that the 40 model rooms changed seasonally. (Davis Hillmer Collection, Courtesy of Detroit Historical Museum.)

10TH FLOOR APPLIANCES. This department built a strong reputation with superior service and depth of selection, offering major brands and its own brands. By the 1960s with specialty chains emerging, the store stepped up their efforts to maintain market share with the famous "You pay no more at Hudson's . . . tell us if we're wrong" campaign. (Davis Hillmer Collection, Courtesy of Detroit Historical Museum.)

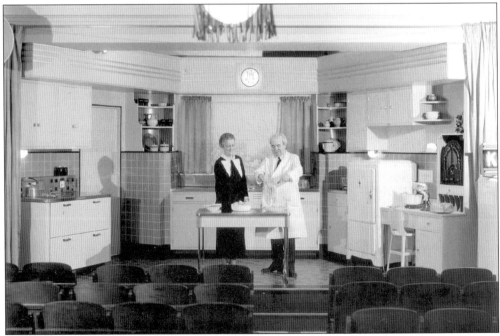

10TH FLOOR MODEL KITCHEN. This was where dream kitchens were born! Guests visited Kitchen Planning to make the most out of their given space. Here, one could view the latest in appliances, floor coverings, counters, cupboards, lighting, and wall coverings. Of course, Hudson's newest recipes were also tested here! (Davis Hillmer Collection, Courtesy of Detroit Historical Museum.)

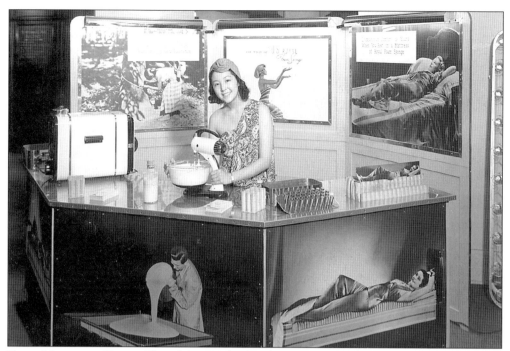

FOAM MATTRESS DEMO. This elaborate display depicts a model demonstrating the attributes of a foam rubber mattress from U.S. Royal. Who could not resist listening to her dialogue, let alone make a purchase! (Davis Hillmer Collection, Courtesy of Detroit Historical Museum.)

SUNBEAM DEMO ON 10TH FLOOR, 1950. There was no more popular small appliance than the classic Sunbeam Mixmaster . . . the first one-stop kitchen appliance. Not to be outdone, Sunbeam toasters also won over June brides with their aesthetic appeal and all-around durability. (Davis Hillmer Collection, Courtesy of Detroit Historical Museum.)

HUDSON'S BASEMENT STORE, C. 1934. Not to be outdone by the "upstairs store," Hudson's Basement (renamed "The Budget Store" in 1961, and in 1973 re-christened "The Rainbow Store"), featured over 60 departments spread out over four acres on two floors. The "store-within-a-store" began in 1914 and was designed to appeal to consumers who desired new well-selected merchandise at popular prices. (Davis Hillmer Collection, Courtesy of Detroit Historical Museum.)

THE POWER OF POPULAR PRICES. The Basement Store had its own merchandising staff, including 105 buyers, and its own advertising and display departments. For many years, the Basement Store did a greater volume of business than any other department store in Michigan, with the exception of Hudson's upstairs store. In fact, the Basement Store actually carried the company through difficult years during World War I and the Great Depression. (Davis Hillmer Collection, Courtesy of Detroit Historical Museum.)

Four

SPECIAL EVENTS AND WINDOW DISPLAYS

DETROIT'S MOST VALUABLE DISPLAY SPACE. Window shopping at the Greater Hudson Store became a spectator sport! Stretching in an unbroken chain along Woodward, Grand River, Farmer, and Gratiot Avenues, Hudson's 49 large display windows dazzled thousands of guests stopping to view bright, colorful merchandise. The above image is from the 1940s. (Davis Hillmer Collection, Courtesy of Detroit Historical Museum.)

VITA RAY CREAM. This elaborate window display was installed for the introduction of Vita Ray, a vitamin cleansing crème from De Mar of Paris. The normal retail price was $1.50 a jar, reduced to $1.00 for this special intro period, c. 1930s. (Davis Hillmer Collection, Courtesy of Detroit Historical Museum.)

PRESSURE COOKERS. The production of pressure cookers was tightly regulated during World War II, as aluminum was needed for the war effort. The pent-up demand following the war created a tremendous craving for quality cookers such as those depicted in the above 1947 window display. (Davis Hillmer Collection, Courtesy of Detroit Historical Museum.)

55TH ANNIVERSARY SALE. In 1936, Hudson's celebrated its 55th anniversary with vibrant exterior displays on the Woodward Building and in the show windows. Full-page ads heralded the drawing power of these once-a-year savings by pulling in guests from throughout Michigan. (Davis Hillmer Collection, Courtesy of Detroit Historical Museum.)

1948 REFRIGERATOR SHOW. In the days before specialized appliance retailers, guests migrated to Hudson's for big ticket purchases. Hudson's staged appliance shows in its auditorium in the same manner as a fashion show. Following frozen food storage in the 1940s, refrigeration technology forged ahead with innovations such as automatic defrost and ice makers. (Davis Hillmer Collection, Courtesy of Detroit Historical Museum.)

1950 WINDOW DISPLAY FOR CHROMCRAFT. This window promoted Chromcraft dinette furniture, which featured chrome tubular legs and formica table tops. Chrome accessories are also represented, as a part of Hudson's annual Housewares Exposition. (Davis Hillmer Collection, Courtesy of Detroit Historical Museum.)

SPRING PLANTING WINDOW, 1950. In today's retail environment, can you imagine devoting an entire window in a prime traffic location to Dutch bulbs? Leave it to Hudson's to accomplish such a feat with this inspiring display and incredible selection! (Davis Hillmer Collection, Courtesy of Detroit Historical Museum.)

LAMPSHADE WINDOW, 1950. Again capitalizing on a new classification, this window heralded the introduction of Glastron lampshades—at the time, a revolutionary form of combined fiberglass and plastic. (Davis Hillmer Collection, Courtesy of Detroit Historical Museum.)

GOOD OLE SUMMERTIME! This popular promotion began in 1961. Glass was removed from eight of the large Woodward windows, and Hudson's installed an Ice Cream Parlor, Root Beer Garden, Candy Store, Grocery Store, Flower Shop, Puppet Show, and Photo Studio. Entertainment included a barbershop quartet and community sing-a-long. And of course, there were stellar sale items! (Courtesy of Detroit Historical Museum.)

LEGO: A TOY FOR TODAY AND TOMORROW. Who knew in the early 1960s that Lego would become the global powerhouse that it is today? This Woodward window depicts the versatility of one's imagination with the various kits available. Better color quality for the Lego bricks was introduced in 1963. (Davis Hillmer Collection, Courtesy of Detroit Historical Museum.)

ESTHER WILLIAMS VISITS. Hudson's was an important stop for visiting dignitaries, film and radio stars, and novelists. In 1951, the 13th Floor dining rooms were filled to capacity for a swimwear fashion show sponsored by Cole of California. Esther Williams and a host of bathing beauties charmed the crowd. (Courtesy of Target Corporation Archives.)

GLORIA SWANSON CREATES BUZZ! In 1952, Hollywood royalty wowed a standing room only crowd on the Sixth Floor as film legend Gloria Swanson promoted a new line of clothing which she designed herself. The year prior, Ms. Swanson was nominated for best actress in *Sunset Boulevard*. (Courtesy of Target Corporation Archives.)

COME JOIN THE CELEBRATION
HERE'S HUDSON'S SALUTE TO THE
INTERNATIONAL FREEDOM FESTIVAL

2 SPECTACULAR AND THRILLING EVENTS

☆ ☆ ☆ FIREWORKS

Saturday, July 2—a gigantic aerial display, cascading 1000 feet or more out of the night skies over Detroit and Windsor. The entire 2½ tons will rocket from the downtown riverfront to create unusual and colorful night-sky effects— many never before seen on this continent. The show all starts at 9:15 p.m.

Hudson's

☆ ☆ LARGEST FLAG

Monday morning, July 4—see Old Glory in all its New Glory. Hudson's will unfurl the World's Largest Flag celebrating our Nation's birthday and the 2nd International Freedom Festival. See this historic FIRST . . . the first official unfurling of the World's Largest Flag as a glorious, big, new 50-star Flag.

. . . In all the World there's nothing like the International Freedom Festival—
in idea, spirit and scope! Hudson's is happy and proud to be a part of it all!

RAIN DATE! IN CASE OF RAIN THE FIREWORKS DISPLAY WILL BE SUNDAY, JULY 3—SAME PLACE.

FREEDOM FESTIVAL FIREWORKS. Hudson's glorious fireworks show began in 1958 as the keystone event of the Detroit-Windsor International Freedom Festival. Up to one million attendees would line both sides of the Detroit River to "ooh and aah" at one of the largest shows of its type in North America. (Courtesy of Central Business District Foundation Archives.)

Little Known Facts About
"THE BIG STORE"

- Did you know that Downtown Hudson's is actually spread out over 32 levels? There are 25 floors, 2 half-floors, a mezzanine, and 4 basements.

- The building rises 410 feet above street level...the tallest department store in the world.

- Total square footage for the Downtown Building is 2,124,316 square feet. Only Macy's 34th Street in New York is larger...by about 26,000 square feet.

- Downtown Hudson's contains one of the largest Otis Elevator Co. installations. There are 51 public passenger elevators, 8 employee passenger elevators, 17 freight elevators, and 48 escalators.

- The largest freight elevator at Hudson's could even accommodate a semi-trailer!

- Detroit Edison maintained 3 transformer centers in the store. Downtown Hudson's generated enough electricity to light up the City of Ypsilanti.

- Did you know there were three 45,000 gallon water tanks (for fire protection) on the 25th Floor of the tower?

- Ever wonder how many "facilities" there were at Hudson's? How about this: 39 men's restrooms, 50 women's restrooms, and 10 private restrooms on the 11th Floor Executive Corridor.

- The largest ladies lounge in the Downtown store was located on the 4th Floor and contained 85 stalls.

- The legendary fur vaults on the 17th Floor could accommodate 83,000 garments. There were actually 3 vaults with three levels of storage in each vault.

- Hudson's actually sits on 11 parcels of land...and, yes, there is a 20 foot alley separating the Woodward Building from the Farmer Street building.

- Electric trucks were used to run between the Main Store and the Beaubien Street Warehouse Complex from the 1920s through the 1950s. (Fire and insurance regulations prohibited the use of gasoline engines on the freight elevators or in the store.)

- The Downtown Store originally boasted of 18 entrances, 49 large display windows, and 50 small display windows...all of which were changed weekly!

- Hudson's set a world's record for the number of fitting rooms in a single store...705!

- The dining rooms and cafeterias served an average of 10,000 meals a day. An additional 6,000 meals a day were served in the Employee's Cafeteria on the 14th Floor.

- Perennial favorite menu items such as chicken pot pie, Maurice Salad, and Canadian Cheese soup debuted in the 13th Floor dining rooms. For many years the ingredients for the Maurice Salad dressing remained a closely guarded Hudson secret!

- The Budget Basement Store was Hudson's closest competition! It was comprised of 2 entire floors, featuring over 60 departments spread out over 4 acres. In its heyday, over 100,000 folks shopped here daily.

- During World War II, the U.S. Government borrowed one of Hudson's giant air-conditioning units for a defense plant, where temperature control was critical. (The store contained one of Carrier Co's. largest air conditioning installations.)

- Hudson's delivery fleet of 350 vehicles annually delivered 10,000 parcels and 900,000 pieces of furniture...and covered 3.2 million miles of metro territory.

- Almost 1,200 Hudsonians served our country during World War II.

- Hudson's was one of the first retailers in the U.S. to clearly mark the price on a given product. (Previously, most stores displayed prices that were coded, so only the clerks knew the actual price.)

- The store offered credit coins, the forerunners to today's credit cards, so guests wouldn't have to carry around large amounts of cash.

- Downtown Hudson's was the first major department store to offer a Bridal Registry.

- Always a frontrunner, Hudson's was one of the first stores to display merchandise in glass front cases, rather than stuffed away in boxes.

- At one time, the Downtown Store boasted of carrying 553,921 items from aspirin to zippers!

- Employment peaked at the Downtown store in the mid-1950s during the holiday season with 12,000 associates working in the building.

- During peak selling seasons, the elevator department employed 125 starters and operators!

- How many electric lights do you think there were in the building? Try 97,000!

- On an average day, despite a Detroit Public Library branch across the street, the Hudson Circulating Library on the Mezzanine handled 600 patrons. This library contained 6,000 volumes...sometimes stocking as many as 450 copies of a single book! (*Gone With the Wind* holds that record!)

- The store Hospital on the 14th Floor was staffed with 4 doctors, 6 nurses and a lab technician.

- Downtown Hudson's holds a number of world's records for single day sales of over $1 million. Many of these records were achieved during the "Downtown Detroit Days" promotions.

- The best year sales-wise for Downtown Hudson's was 1954. The store topped $155 million in sales. Imagine that in today's dollars!

- Hudson's was the first department store to offer a personal shopper.

- Hudson's built a massive merchandising network...dealing with 28,000 vendors in 10,000 cities.

What merchandise and service functi
Let us freshe

This is a compilation of departmental listings, combining list

MAIN FLOOR
Fine/Costume Jewelry
Handbags/Small Leather Goods
Cosmetics
Women's Gloves/Belts
Hosiery
Umbrellas
Women's Neckwear
Men's Underwear and Socks
Men's Pajamas
Men's Dress and Sport Shirts
Men's Neckwear and Suspenders
Men's Gloves/Hosiery
Smoke Shop
Men's Belts and Umbrellas

In the Farmer St. Building:
Miss Detroiter Sportswear
Marketplace
Marketplace Foods and Candy
Wine Shop
Valet Parking

MEZZANINE
Luggage
Party Favors and Paper Goods
Greeting Cards
Table Novelties
Adult Games
Puzzle Library
Books and Magazines
Circulating Library
(Replaced in 1954 with
Stamps and Coins)
Stationery and Engraving
Gifts and Clocks
Pharmacy
Personal Shopping Service
Public Lockers
American Express Office
Post Office
Check Room
Optical Service
Baked Goods
Mezzanine Tea Room *(Later Buffeteria)*
Soda Fountain

SECOND FLOOR
Sporting Goods
Golf Shop
Ski Shop
Young Men's Clothing

Men's Sport Clothing
Men's Suits
Kuppenheimer Shop
University Shop
Men's Topcoats and Overcoats
Uniforms
Men's Shoes
Men's Robes and Housecoats
Men's Hats and Caps
Custom Tailoring
Ask Mr. Foster Travel Bureau
Cameras and Supplies
Kodascope Library *(Film Rental)*
Men's Will Call Desk

THIRD FLOOR
Ribbons
Blankets, Spreads and Comforters
Sheets and Pillow Cases
Towels and Wash Cloths
Table Linens
Art Needlework
Notions
Instructions in Needlework and
  Lampshade Making
Gift Novelties
Pillows
Fabrics and Patterns
Hosiery, Zipper and Glove Repair
Glove Cleaning and Re-weaving
Artificial Flowers
Hudson's Sewing Center
Dry Cleaning

FOURTH FLOOR
Girl's Clothing
Girl Scout Uniforms
Boy's Clothing
Boy Scout Uniforms
Infant's Department
Infant's Medical Supplies
Advisory Service to Expectant Mothers
Nursery Furniture
Model Nursery Rooms
Women's Lounge and Writing Lounge
Children's Changing Room
Tourneur Powder Blending Salon
Baby Carriages
O'Connor Portrait Studio
Public Telephones
Sub Teen Shop

FIFTH FLOOR
High School Shop
Equestrienne Shop
Sports Accessories
Hoover/Wash Dress Section
Aprons
Knit, Silk and Muslin Underwear
The Lingerie Shop
Pajamas
Corsets
Brassieres
Junior Miss Shop *(Later years,*
  A Nice Girl Like You)

SIXTH FLOOR
Nurses and Maids Uniforms
Inexpensive Coats
Women's Suits
Negligees and Bathrobes
Furs
Misses and Women's Moderate Dresses
Casual Shop
Bridal Secretary
Bridal Gowns
Evening Gowns and Wraps
Women's and Misses Inexpensive Dresses

SEVENTH FLOOR
Woodward Shops
Women's and Misses Millinery
The French Room
Dobbs' Sport Shop
Women's and Misses Shoes
Shoe Repair
Shoe Shining
Untrimmed Hats and Trimmings
Shoe Adjustment
Women's and Misses Better Coats
Women's and Misses Better Dresses
Women's and Misses Better Suits
Old Print Shop *(Later moved to 3rd Floor)*
J. L. Hudson Gallery
  (Later Detroit Artists Market)

EIGHTH FLOOR
Home Planning Center
Young Housekeepers Bureau
Drapery Department
Upholstery and Drapery Fabric
Chintz Shop
Pillow Shop
Tapestries
Studio of Interior Decoration

Closet Shop
Curtain Hardware
Window and Porch Shades
Folding Screens
Oriental Rugs
Carpet Rooms
Domestic Rugs and Carpets
Linoleum Shop

NINTH FLOOR
Furniture
Model Rooms
Springs and Mattresses
Furniture Adjustment
Mirrors
Card Tables

TENTH FLOOR
Baskets
Bathroom Equipment
Birds and Bird Cages
Electrical Appliances
Model Kitchens
Home Service Bureau
Fireplace Fixtures
Kitchen Equipment
Plants, Bulbs, Shrubs and Trees
Heating Appliances
Sewing Machines
Stoves, Gas and Electric Ranges
Unpainted Furniture
Washing Machines and Ironers
Electrical Refrigerators
Wedding Gift Consultant
China
Glassware
Customer Service
Collector's Gallery
Gift Wrap

ELEVENTH FLOOR
Lamps
Office Furniture
Cashier's Office
Credit Office
Research Office
Pictures
Contract Department
Extended Payment Office
Lost and Found
Executive Offices
Buyer's Clerical Office

were performed on all of those floors?
our memory!

he store in its heyday to more modern functions and activities.

WELFTH FLOOR
erations
sheling Room *(Men's Alterations)*
ll Call Office
reau of Adjustments
in and Little Auditoriums
ys (Later moved to Four)
y Advisory Bureau
ist Supplies
rdware and Paints
ntaland
Children Only Shop
ildren's Snack Shop
iday Carnival
yaway
ols
ys
me Furnishings Clearance Center
S. Computer Center

HIRTEENTH FLOOR
cutive Dining Room
Pine Room Restaurant
Georgian Room Restaurant
Early American Room Restaurant
*later years these became
he Riverview Room and Beef Emporium)*
sic Store
nos and Musical Instruments
et Music and Music Rolls
rolas
ords
*later years music moved to 11 and
en to the Mezzanine. Originally was in
e former Good Housekeeping Building
Library Street)*
's and Women's Recreation Rooms
porate Store Planning/Architecture
tral Kitchens/Candy
efit Office

URTEENTH FLOOR
erintendent's Offices
loyment Office
mation Office
ection Office
loyee's Cafeteria
pital
ator Supervisor's Office and
erators Lounge
's Hat Cleaning
ence Pay Office

Public Lockers
Salon Americana Beauty Salons
Children's Barber Shop
Executive Barber Shop
Corporate Human Resources

FIFTEENTH FLOOR
Receiving, Marking and Stock Rooms
Visual Merchandising *(Display)*
Gift Basket Assembly
Central Gift Wrap

FIFTEEN AND
ONE-HALF FLOOR
Document Storage
Receiving

SIXTEENTH FLOOR
Receiving and Marking Rooms
Invoice Office
Import Office
Buyer's Offices
Carpenter Shop
Sample Offices
Jewelry Repair
Accounts Payable
Glass Shop

SEVENTEENTH FLOOR
Fur Storage
Fur Will Call and Repairs
Central Order Board
Cash Register Repair
World Wide Insurance
Paint Shop
Elevator Penthouse

EIGHTEENTH FLOOR
Sales Audit
  (Pneumatic tube system ended here)
Paymaster's Office
Engine Room
Store Rooms

NINETEENTH FLOOR
Advertising
Sales Promotion
Public Relations
Advertising Accounting Office
Downtown Training Room
Video Production
Hudsonian Office
Advertising Photo Studio

TWENTIETH FLOOR
Supply Department
Purchasing
Main Switchboard
Telephone Equipment Room
Package Development Center
Carillon
Telephone Order Board
Mail Order

TWENTY-FIRST FLOOR
Store Laundry

TWENTY-ONE AND
ONE-HALF FLOOR
Corporate Sign Shop
Corporate Print Shop

TWENTY-SECOND FLOOR
Elevator Maintenance

TWENTY-THIRD FLOOR
Mechanical Equipment

TWENTY-FOURTH FLOOR
Executive Health Spa
Executive Squash Court
Hot Water Tanks

TWENTY-FIFTH FLOOR
Door access to wraparound neon sign
Water Tanks

THE BASEMENT STORE
FIRST BASEMENT
Blouses and Sweaters
Boys' Clothing and Furnishings
Candy and Nuts
Corsets
Girls' and Juniors Apparel
Handkerchiefs and Neckwear
Leather Goods and Jewelry
Luggage
Men's Clothing
Men's Furnishings and Hats
Men's Shoes
Men's Work Clothing
O'Connor Photo Studio
Toilet Goods and Drugs
Men's and Boys' Will Call
Women's Larger Sizes Apparel
Women's and Misses Coats and Furs
Women's and Misses Dresses and Suits
Women's and Children's Hosiery
Women's and Children's Millinery
Women's Underwear
Women's Silk, Cotton and Muslin
Underwear

SECOND BASEMENT
Art Goods
Notions
Hemstitching
Awnings and Venetian Blinds
Blankets and Bedding
Boys' and Girls' Shoes
Draperies and Curtains
Gift Novelties
Infants' and Children's Wear
Lamps
Linings
Luncheonette
Patterns
Robes and Negligees
Rugs and Coverings
Silks and Woolens
Wash Dresses and Aprons
Wash Linens and Fabrics
Will Call
Women's Shoes

THIRD BASEMENT
Electrician's Room
Basement Sign Department
Cash Tube Room
Receiving and Marking Rooms
Stock Rooms
Engine Room
Maintenance Department

FOURTH BASEMENT
Orderly Department
Basement Display
Packing Department
Incinerator
Marking Rooms
Return Goods Room
Delivery

ADDITIONAL
DOWNTOWN FACILITIES
• 4 Warehouses bounded by
  Madison, Brush, Adams
• 1 Warehouse on West Fort Street
  at Rosa Parks
• Shoppers' Parking Garage on
  Broadway at Grand River *(Now known
  as the Opera House Garage)*
• Hudson's Downtown Tire and Auto
  Center On Monroe Street at Randolph
  (In the Parking Garage)
  Tires moved here from the Second Floor
  of the store

HUDSON'S EXHIBIT. In August of 1997, the Detroit Historical Museum opened its major exhibition, "Remembering Downtown Hudson's." The popular exhibit ran for two years. Images can be seen on the Detroit Historical Museum website at www.detroithistorical.org.

DOWNTOWN DETROIT DAYS, 1970s. In April of 1922, 13 Motor City business people met at the invitation of Oscar Webber, then CEO of Hudson's, to create an organization to investigate unfair tax assessments and to encourage the construction of a rapid rail line. This is how the Central Business District Association was born. CBDA regularly organized and promoted some of downtown's most successful events including DDDays. (Courtesy of Central Business District Foundation Archives.)

Hudson's DDD Savings Celebration

Monday, Tuesday and Wednesday, May 18 through 20, Hudson's joins in celebrating the 10th anniversary of Downtown Detroit Days. A raft of important values await budget-conscious shoppers on practically every floor of the Downtown store. Come in often. Join the fun, get in on the savings, try your luck at the prizes. You'll enjoy every minute of this big event.

Win a week for two in Paris! Fly TWA, all expenses paid

This special 10th-birthday prize features a week for two in Paris. All arrangements made by Hudson's Ask Mr. Foster travel service. How to win? Just write about an experience in Downtown Detroit—real or make-believe. Second prize— a real estate lot in Florida—courtesy General Development Corp. and CBDA—plus a trip for two to Florida. Get the details on coupons at Hudson's Downtown.

You can win important prizes, each and every day

A new 1964 Plymouth Savoy, awarded through CBDA and the Greater Detroit Plymouth Dealers. A swimming pool, an RCA Victor color TV, a gas dryer, an electric range, many other prizes awarded each DDDay. Easy to enter. Just fill out an entry blank and drop it in one of the boxes on Hudson's First Floor or on the site of the Old City Hall.

HUDSON'S

DDDAYS AD. Downtown Detroit Days provided Hudson's with phenomenal traffic and sales twice a year, in April and October. The Central Business District Association began DDDays in 1954 to promote a positive image of downtown through special events and retail programs. (Courtesy of Central Business District Foundation Archives.)

Five

PATRIOTISM

THE WAR YEARS. Publicity by Hudson's for the World War II effort was unprecedented. All-out support was provided on behalf of the United States Treasury Department, the National War Fund, and the Armed Services. Countless elaborate window displays, full-page newspaper ads, and 12th Floor Auditorium spectacles promoted war bonds. The image above depicts a 1943 window display. (Davis Hillmer Collection, Courtesy of Detroit Historical Museum.)

PULLING OUT ALL THE STOPS. This 1943 window display promotes the "Four Freedoms War Bond Show." This was a massive event presented by the United States Treasury Department and the *Saturday Evening Post* and co-sponsored by Hudson's. The objective was to achieve record-breaking war bond sales. The event included personal appearances by Gloria Swanson and Victor Mature, as well as the display of the original Norman Rockwell paintings depicting "The Four Freedoms." (Davis Hillmer Collection, Courtesy of Detroit Historical Museum.)

FOUR FREEDOMS AUDITORIUM EXHIBIT AND SHOW. Besides the program presented in Hudson's 12th Floor Auditorium, a massive parade down Woodward marked the formal opening of "Four Freedoms," which brought a spectacular array of uniforms to Detroit, from all branches of the service. A reviewing stand on Hudson's marquee was filled with notables as the governor officially opened the program. (Davis Hillmer Collection, Courtesy of Detroit Historical Museum.)

AMERICAN LEGION FLAG. This enormous flag, seven stories tall on the Woodward side of the store, greeted the American Legion during its Detroit convention in 1931. (Davis Hillmer Collection, Courtesy of Detroit Historical Museum.)

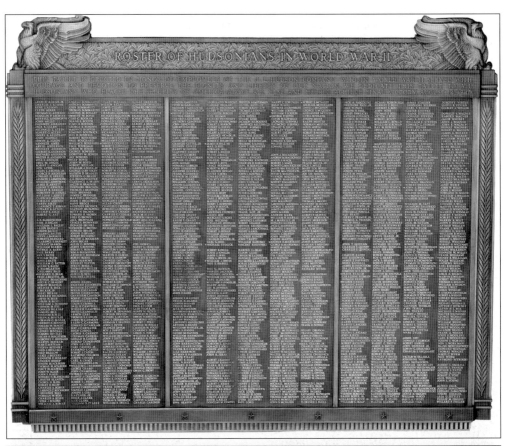

Opposite, above: **SACRIFICES REMEMBERED.** In 1947, Hudson's commissioned an elaborate plaque that was prominently displayed at the Grand River escalators on the Main Floor. The names of all 1,446 Hudson's employees who served their country during World War II are inscribed. Thirty-one of the names on the plaque are preceded by a star, to denote Hudson's employees who died in service. In 1993, this plaque was moved to Hudson's Northland and re-dedicated. (Davis Hillmer Collection, Courtesy of Detroit Historical Museum.)

Opposite, below: **VICTORY DAY PREPARATIONS.** Hudson's celebrated Victory Day in 1945 with a spectacular display of patriotism on the Woodward façade of the store. A huge "V" featuring images of troops was flanked by hundreds of American flags. All 49 main floor display windows were also devoted to Victory Day. (Davis Hillmer Collection, Courtesy of Detroit Historical Museum.)

WAC RECRUITMENT AT HUDSON'S. In 1942, the Women's Army Auxiliary Corps was established. By 1944, the first WACs arrived in North Africa, followed by arrivals in the Pacific and Normandy. Countless women served stateside in all branches of the service and relieved men for combat duty overseas. The above image depicts a WAC recruiter on the Main Floor. (Davis Hillmer Collection, Courtesy of Detroit Historical Museum.)

HUDSON'S AIR CONDITIONING IS DRAFTED. In 1943, half of the equipment that cooled 11 out of 15 floors at Downtown Hudson's was borrowed by the United States Government for the war effort. The Hudson refrigeration equipment of 1,500 tons capacity was moved to an airplane engine factory for mass production of precision parts. (Courtesy of Target Corporation Archives.)

WAR BONDS SOLD AT HUDSON'S. Hudson's was the first retail operation in the United States authorized to sell bonds directly to employees and guests. In 1945, the store was recognized by the U.S. Treasury for selling more individual E-bonds than any other retailer: 500,000 bonds! (Courtesy of Target Corporation Archives.)

Opposite: **IT'S A GRAND OLD FLAG!** Depicted at right is the 1949 flag dedication, which required a crew of 55 individuals to handle the seven-story flag. Guinness proclaimed the Hudson flag to be "the world's largest." To maintain this title, various sections were added to the flag, and in 1960, stars were added for Hawaii and Alaska. Following the final public appearance for this beloved flag during America's bicentennial in 1976, Hudson's donated it to the Smithsonian Institution. (Courtesy of Target Corporation Archives.)

SALUTING OUR FLAG. One of the most heartwarming Hudson's traditions occurred each Flag Day with the unfurling of Old Glory, high above Woodward Avenue. This grand tradition began on Armistice Day in 1923. A replacement flag debuted in 1949. The above 1923 image looks south on Woodward. (Courtesy of Target Corporation Archives.)

*H*udson's proudly displays

the world's largest flag

**READ THE INTERESTING STORY OF THIS FAMOUS
BANNER THAT GREW TO BE SEVEN STORIES TALL**

DIMENSIONS
FOR THE
WORLD'S
LARGEST
FLAG.

Size:
104 feet by
235 feet

Weight:
Approximately
1,500 pounds

Size of stars:
5.5 feet wide

Size of stripes:
8 feet wide

Materials:
2,715 yards of
shrink-proof
Army wool
3,840 yards of
thread
2,988 feet of
webbing
6,240 feet of
snow-white
nylon rope

Manufacturer:
George P.
Johnson
Company,
Detroit,
Michigan.

HUDSON'S FLAG STANDS PROUD AT THIRD WAR LOAN RALLY. The $15 billion goal of the Third War Loan meant that the record amount of bonds sold in a single month would have to be more than doubled and over 40 million American citizens would have to invest in a $100 Series E Savings Bond. Over 152,000 advertisements were placed in newspapers (and Hudson's placed many!) to promote the drive between September 9, 1943 and October 2, 1943. (Courtesy of Detroit Historical Museum.)

AERIAL VIEW OF HUDSON'S FLAG IN 1949. The long and eventful history of Hudson's original 1923 flag included displays at the U.S. Capitol in 1929 and at the New York World's Fair in 1939. The "new" 1949 flag was in production for six months. To complete it, eight women worked at sewing machines for more than 700 hours. Three sailmakers put in the webbing, ropes, and metal eyes for the ropes. (Courtesy of Target Corporation Archives.)

Six

EXTRAORDINARY SERVICES AND ASSOCIATES

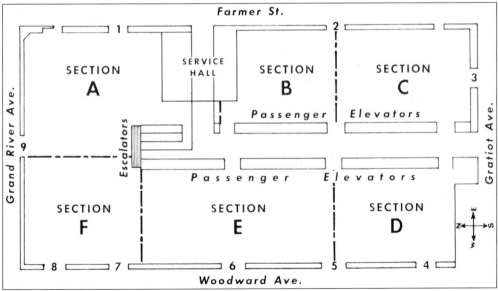

EXTRAORDINARY SERVICES. Guest services were a time-honored tradition at Hudson's. The diverse ways that guests needed these services underscored the versatility of "the big store." Just think of the convenience and time saved by utilizing these services . . . all under one roof! Instead of having to remember the names of streets, a new store directory (above) was devised that divided the store into six sections. Guests could now plan their shopping trip by the first six letters of the alphabet. (Courtesy of Target Corporation Archives.)

BEAUTY SALON, 1947. Hudson's Beauty Salon initially occupied 17,000 square feet on the Woodward side of the Seventh Floor and was decorated in a Spanish motif. The salon employed 160 operators and included rooms for facials, complexion consultations, make-up artists, and something new for that time: permanent waves. (Davis Hillmer Collection, Courtesy of Detroit Historical Museum.)

HUDSON'S CONTRACT DIVISION. This lucrative division of the company moved to renovated quarters on the 13th Floor in 1963. Many companies, large and small, utilized the services of this division for the purchase of office furniture, carpeting, draperies, and office design services. At one time, Hudson's was one of Steelcase Corporation's largest vendors in the state. (Courtesy of Target Corporation Archives.)

CIRCUS LAND: A MOST UNIQUE BARBER SHOP. One of the most endearing memories of the downtown store for many folks was the Children's Barbershop, initially located in the Farmer Building on the Fourth Floor. This unique barbershop was furnished and arranged like an animal circus, with 15 chairs and 15 barbers for hair cutting. (Courtesy of Target Corporation Archives.)

A CUT AND A SHOW! In front of each chair was a miniature stage. Every 60 seconds, the scene changed, culminating with a series of 15 paintings. The adjoining waiting room was covered with a large circus canopy and featured fanciful latticed windows. It also had a wonderful peep show with more marionettes. The slogan for the barbershop was, "from now on, the day of the haircut is going to be a great holiday!" (Courtesy of Target Corporation Archives.)

Opposite: **TOURNEUR POWDER BLENDING SALON.** This airy hideaway was ensconced on the Fourth Floor of the Farmer Building. Tourneur face powder was individually blended for guests on the spot. It retailed for $3 a box. (Davis Hillmer Collection, Courtesy of Detroit Historical Museum.)

OUR ANIMALS ARE CHILD-FRIENDLY. Each chair represented a different animal. The following animals were represented: elephant, moose, bull, lion, buffalo, tiger, bison, bear, and giraffe. In later years, the Children's Barber Shop moved to the 14th Floor and become more non-descript. (Courtesy of Target Corporation Archives.)

GETTING TOTALLY PAMPERED. A staff of seven trained associates would cater to each guest's specification at the Tourneur Salon. Hudson's boasted the largest-volume cosmetic division of any department store in the nation. Top brands from the 1950s such as Estee Lauder, Revlon, Elizabeth Arden, and Chanel are still prevalent today. (Courtesy of Manning Brothers.)

MEN'S BARBER SHOP. Hudson's hair care for men initially consisted of a barber shop with 10 attendants. This image depicts the barber shop prior to the advent of central air conditioning. Note all of the fans on the ledges. In later years, the barber shop became part of Salon Americana, a unisex salon. (Davis Hillmer Collection, Courtesy of Detroit Historical Museum.)

THAT'S A LOT OF POLISH! Hudson's Shoeshine was located on the Mezzanine. There were 16 stations positioned on black and white tiles, surrounded by a marble base. Hudson's Shoe Repair, first opened in 1935, handled 2,500 guests each week. The shoe repair was staffed with 25 associates and also re-built shoes, dyed leathers and fabrics, and cleaned and restored soiled footwear. (Davis Hillmer Collection, Courtesy of Detroit Historical Museum.)

ASK MR. FOSTER TRAVEL SERVICE. This travel service was a national franchise that opened a branch on the Second Floor of Hudson's in 1924. Each staff member had to complete a six-month training course before being qualified as a representative of Ask Mr. Foster. This service was a terrific resource for vacation ideas and catered to all budgets. (Davis Hillmer Collection, Courtesy of Detroit Historical Museum.)

TYPING LESSONS. What better way for Hudson's to market typewriters to guests than to offer free typing lessons? By the 1920s, most typewriter models featured a common keyboard. Printing transpired through a ribbon using one shift key and four banks of keys. This made typing more accessible for the public. (Davis Hillmer Collection, Courtesy of Detroit Historical Museum.)

CIRCULATING LIBRARY. Despite the fact that the downtown branch of the Detroit Public Library was across the street, Hudson's Circulating Library was a very popular spot on the Mezzanine. The rental fee in 1951 was 3¢ per book. This library employed a staff of five, averaged 600 guests a day, and was stocked with 6,000 volumes. (Courtesy of Target Corporation Archives.)

HUDSON'S BOOK DEPARTMENT. The Mezzanine Book Department was arguably the most popular department in the store for many guests. Through the years, the store held book fairs and lectures, and hosted many prominent authors for signings. The department also featured the largest selection of magazines in town. (Brochures Courtesy of Michael Hauser.)

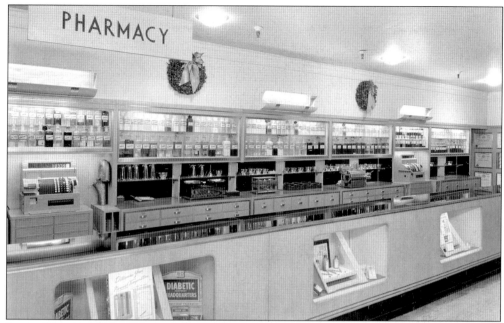

LONG BEFORE EVERY CORNER HAD A DRUG STORE. Hudson's Pharmacy opened on the Mezzanine in 1934. By the 1950s there were over 1 million prescriptions on file, with an average of 500 prescriptions filled daily. The pharmacy staff consisted of 30 associates, including 18 registered pharmacists. Due to the large number of immigrant guests, the staff could also communicate in German, Italian, Polish, and French. (Davis Hillmer Collection, Courtesy of Detroit Historical Museum.)

SELF-SERVICE PARKING AT HUDSON'S. In the autumn of 1957, Hudson's converted their Shoppers' Parking Garage over to a self-serve format. (This garage at Broadway and John R. is known today as the Opera House Garage.) The new service was promoted as being quieter and smoother operating, with less chance of having fenders dented! (Courtesy of Target Corporation Archives.)

PHOTO STUDIO. The O'Connor Studios maintained locations in the First Basement and on the Second Floor. Here one could arrange for wedding photos, studio portraits, or even have passport photos taken. The studios also specialized in framing, re-touching old photos, color tinting black and white images, and enlarging. (Davis Hillmer Collection, Courtesy of Detroit Historical Museum.)

THE GENERAL OFFICE FLOOR. This image depicts the Credit Office on the 11th Floor. Here one could pay his or her monthly charge coin statement, cash checks, purchase savings bonds, and make layaway payments. Other functions in this portion of the Woodward Building were offices for the Controller and Cashiers' Office. The Farmer Building on this floor housed the Executive Offices. (Davis Hillmer Collection, Courtesy of Detroit Historical Museum.)

FOR THE BRIDE. Hudson's Bridal Registry was established in 1941 on the 10th Floor. The store's bridal gift secretary assisted guests with shower plans and gift selections free of charge. By 1957, Hudson's was registering over 10,000 brides a year . . . one-third of all brides in Wayne County! (Davis Hillmer Collection, Courtesy of Detroit Historical Museum.)

INTERIOR DESIGN. Hudson's Studio of Interior Design, as depicted in the 1953 image above, was located on the Eighth Floor. This full-service studio offered guests one-stop shopping for furniture, fabrics, floor coverings, window treatments, lighting, and fine art for homes throughout Michigan. Store designers also had access to showrooms not open to the public. (Davis Hillmer Collection, Courtesy of Detroit Historical Museum.)

HOME ADVISORY BUREAU. This valuable service, located on the 10th Floor, could answer questions on everything from how to remove spots to how to freeze eggs. A staff of trained home economists was eager to please any guest or respond to any challenge. (Courtesy of Michael Hauser.)

HOME PLANNING CENTER, 10TH FLOOR. Yet another unique service combined the knowledge, skill, and experience of nationally-renowned architects with Hudson's own associates trained to assist those planning to purchase, renovate, or build a home. Guests could peruse listings of over 1,400 homes for sale in metro Detroit and purchase blueprints for $5. (Courtesy of Target Corporation Archives.)

AUDITORIUM EVENTS. The 12th Floor Auditorium was a virtual "civic center" for the community. Thousands of Michiganders attended auto shows, flower exhibitions, quilt shows, dog shows, and Toytown/Santaland extravaganzas. The 1941 image above depicts a British Import Fair. (Davis Hillmer Collection, Courtesy of Detroit Historical Museum.)

RE-INVENTING THE AUDITORIUM. The auditorium originally consisted of two exhibit halls. In 1956, both were gutted and joined as one to create a 10,000-square-foot hall. The renovated space featured flexible lighting, natural oak walls, handsome draperies, excellent acoustics, and backstage dressing rooms. (Davis Hillmer Collection, Courtesy of Detroit Historical Museum.)

MMMMM GOOD! The Candy Department was established at Hudson's in 1942. The war years and the consequent shortages of sugar and chocolate slowed the flow of candy to the store. Candy was featured at several outposts including the Main Floor, Fourth Floor, and First Basement, as depicted in the above 1953 image. (Courtesy Target Corporation Archives.)

THIRST QUENCHER. Long before it became fashionable to have juice bars, there was Hudson's right at the forefront! The Orange Punch Department opened in 1931 and was located in the First Basement. It was a popular stop for both shoppers and employees. More than 30,000 gallons were consumed monthly. That's a lot of Vitamin C! (Courtesy of Target Corporation Archives.)

BASEMENT STORE CAFETERIA. The cafeteria located in the Second Basement opened in 1928 as the Basement Tea Room. In 1947, it was converted over to cafeteria-style dining. This restaurant and the Mezzanine Tea Room would annually handle one million more guest transactions than the dining rooms on the 13th Floor. (Davis Hillmer Collection, Courtesy of Detroit Historical Museum.)

MEZZANINE SODA FOUNTAIN. In 1928, Hudson's elegant soda fountain opened, complete with architectural ornamentation such as detailed plaster and hand-painted tiles. In 1951, the fountain introduced automatic counter service. A conveyor with an electronic eye transmitted orders to the kitchen. Located adjacent to the fountain was the Mezzanine Tea Room. (Davis Hillmer Collection, Courtesy of Detroit Historical Museum.)

THE GEORGIAN DINING ROOM, 13TH FLOOR. The formal dining rooms were formerly located on the Seventh Floor and simply known as "The Café." When the Greater Hudson addition opened in 1928, these restaurants were relocated to the 13th Floor, creating three distinct dining options. The Georgian Room, shown above, featured an elegant atmosphere with hand-painted murals and floral window treatments. (Davis Hillmer Collection, Courtesy Detroit Historical Museum.)

THE EARLY AMERICAN DINING ROOM, 13TH FLOOR. This dining room was airy and lighter in appearance with hints of elegance such as mirrors and chandeliers. This room was reserved for those who did not smoke. Low-calorie menus were introduced in 1955, and by 1970, one could order his or her favorite cocktail. (Davis Hillmer Collection, Courtesy Detroit Historical Museum.)

THE PINE ROOM, 13TH FLOOR. This dining area resembled a library with beautifully-paneled walls and deep green accents. In 1959, this room was renovated so it could be divided into three rooms and thus be utilized by organizations for meetings. In 1975, this space became the Beef Emporium, a popular businessmen's luncheon spot. (Davis Hillmer Collection, Courtesy of Detroit Historical Museum.)

THE RIVERVIEW ROOM, 13TH FLOOR. In 1959, the Georgian and Early American Rooms were combined to create the Riverview Room. Four large picture windows on the east side of the room (Farmer Street) provided breathtaking views of the Detroit River. Two large contemporary murals by Birmingham artist Richard Jennings covered the north and south walls. (Davis Hillmer Collection, Courtesy of Detroit Historical Museum.)

13TH FLOOR DINING ROOM MENU, C. 1941. The Foods Division was always an integral part of Hudson's. Some of our favorite recipes were born at the downtown store. Ahh! The aroma of those wonderful blueberry muffins, the sensation of biting into the first helping of chicken pot pie, wondering about that secret recipe for Maurice Salad, or savoring the delicious Canadian Cheese soup! (Courtesy of Michael Hauser.)

PLEASE DON'T TAKE MY STROLLER

MY MOMMY AND I ARE EATING IN HUDSON'S DINING ROOM

Hudson's Happy Holiday Menu

An American Tradition

ROAST SLICED BREAST OF TURKEY · over savory dressing with country gravy, mashed potatoes, vegetable, cranberry sauce, served with Hudson's roll and butter, 4.25

A Holiday Treat

CHICKEN WALDORF SALAD - new from Hudson's kitchen - our special Waldorf made with breast of chicken, apples, celery and walnuts served with tomato slices and garnished with egg quarters, a freshly baked muffin too, 3.95

CROISSANT AU FROMAGE - a flaky buttery croissant filled with sliced breast of turkey and sliced ham, covered with bubbling cheese sauce with bacon, served with cranberry orange relish, 3.95

Ours Alone

CARAMEL APPLE SUNDAE - vanilla ice cream crowned with caramel sauce, apples and walnuts, 1.50

Holiday Pick-Ups

HOLLY HOPPER - a blend of creme de menthe (non-alcoholic), vanilla ice cream and milk, 1.75

CRANBERRY WHIRL - cranberry and lime juice blended with vanilla yogurt for a refreshing moment in your busy day, 1.75

Dessert Treats For All From Our Bakery

OLD FASHION PLUM PUDDING - with rum hard sauce and brandied country sauce, 1.35

A WEDGE OF PUMPKIN PIE - frosted with whipped cream, 1.25

ENGLISH TRIFLE - merry old England's holiday delight, 1.50

Take The Holiday Home

HUDSON'S FRUIT CAKE ·
One Pound, 6.00
Two Pounds, 12.00

PLUM PUDDING ·
One Pound, 3.45

HARD SAUCE ·
6 oz. 1.75

All made in our own bakery.
For sale at the Cashier.

THOSE BUSY KITCHENS. At peak times during the holidays, 10,000 meals a day were served in Hudson's restaurants. Another 6,000 meals were served in the spacious Employee Cafeteria on the 14th Floor. Hudson's had an extensive Pantry Shop and Bakery, and was one of the first stores to feature a Cheese Shop and a Health Foods department. Additionally, the store housed the Candy Kitchens and the Wine Cellar. (Courtesy of Michael Hauser.)

THE HUDSON CAROLERS. This group of 60 voices strong began delighting guests with glorious holiday songs in 1930. They could be seen daily, performing in various areas throughout the store. The carolers wore beautiful holly red robes and presented a repertoire of standard carols and hymns. For those who could not make it downtown, the carolers in later years performed on WWJ radio and television. (Courtesy of Target Corporation Archives.)

THE SUNSHINE SINGERS. Another guest favorite were the Sunshine Singers, formed in 1955. This inspirational group of 25 women were members of Hudson's Housekeeping Department. Many of these women sang in their respective church choirs. Guests and employees looked forward to their in-store concerts as well as those performed at the Art Institute Auditorium, which benefited music education. (Courtesy Target Corporation Archives.)

MARGARET HAYES.
Miss Hayes was a
longtime editor
of the *Hudsonian*,
Hudson's award-
winning in-
house employee
publication. Hayes
tirelessly covered
new store openings,
special events, and
heart-warming
conversations with
retirees. In later
years, she also
assisted with "Open
Line," an internal
communications
program.
(Courtesy of
Target Corporation
Archives.)

NAMON CLARKE.
Mr. Clarke's career at
Hudson's spanned 32
years. He began as an
elevator starter, later
became superintendent
of passenger elevators
and escalators, and
retired as credit
union manager. He
was instrumental in
breaking the color
barrier at Hudson's,
paving the way for
African Americans
to enter sales and
management positions.
(Courtesy of Target
Corporation Archives.)

FRED WILKINS. Mr. Wilkins was instrumental in planning Hudson's physical growth. For 32 years he served as the store architect and as building superintendent. Outstanding examples of his forward thinking include the implementation of an open floor plan, the use of natural light and color, and the introduction of mass displays. (Courtesy of Target Corporation Archives.)

RICHARD HIRN. Mr. Hirn was Hudson's special effects artist whose creativity was visible throughout the company. He created matchbook covers, *Hudsonian* magazine covers, tissue boxes, posters, menus, catalog covers, and special event banners. Some of his best work appeared during Hudson's 75th anniversary. (Courtesy of Target Corporation Archives.)

Seven

THE GRAND DAME WINDS DOWN

BREATHING NEW LIFE INTO 1206 WOODWARD. In the 1970s, Hudson's Downtown was faced with dramatic changes in the retail industry and in the shopping habits of their guests. An aggressive remodeling plan in 1974 provided nearly one additional decade of life for the Grand Dame of Woodward Avenue retailing. (Courtesy of Target Corporation Archives.)

A Browser's Paradise. Long a favorite of downtowners, the expansive Book Department on the Mezzanine, was, for many years, the largest bookstore in town. This department also featured a broad magazine section. Even during the mid-1970s, this department had the highest volume of sales for all Hudson's locations. (Courtesy of Target Corporation Archives.)

Relocating Departments. The 1970s brought departmental relocations, designed to maximize space allocations in the store. Golf and Tennis moved to a bright spot on the Second Floor. Many of the large street-level display windows were sealed off, and Hudson's attempted to rent office space in unused portions of the Farmer Building. (Courtesy of Target Corporation Archives.)

THE CHILDREN'S FLOOR. In 1974 the "Little Miss Hudson" boutique debuted on the Fourth Floor. Classifications that complemented each other were relocated closer to one another, such as Toys moving from the 12th Floor to the Fourth Floor. To better accommodate weekend shoppers, the downtown store added Sunday holiday hours in 1972. (Courtesy of Target Corporation Archives.)

THE FASHION FLOORS. The 1970s saw a new Contemporary Collections area (left) on the Sixth Floor and a large area devoted to Juniors on the Fifth Floor, called "A Nice Girl Like You." Miss Detroiter Sportswear moved to a new home on the Main Floor of the Farmer Building. (Courtesy of Target Corporation Archives.)

HOME FURNISHINGS RELOCATIONS. In 1974, the entire 10th Floor was renovated for housewares, gifts, appliances, silver, china, hardware, and the like. Three years later, many of these departments moved to the Main Floor of the Farmer Building as part of a new lifestyle concept known as "Marketplace." (Courtesy of Target Corporation Archives.)

RENOVATIONS DOWN UNDER. In the 1970s, "The Rainbow Store," formerly known as the Budget Store, also received new fixtures and carpeting. The Second Basement was closed briefly, but re-opened as a Budget Home Store. Many special events including fashion shows and product demonstrations were scheduled for a popular "Friday" series. (Courtesy Target Archives.)

A FINAL RIDE. These shoppers were some of the last to escalate to various floors for last-minute purchases. The downtown store closed its doors for good in January of 1983. Management did not alert the media, as they wanted the Grand Dame of Detroit retailing to close with dignity. (Courtesy of Douglas Peters.)

DOWNTOWN'S FAVORITE NOONTIME STOP. The Mezzanine was a favorite destination for many downtown workers, especially on a cold or rainy day. Where else, on one floor, could one shop, dine, browse for books, select music, visit a pharmacy, grab an ice cream cone, or view stamps and coins from around the world? (Courtesy of Douglas Peters.)

SANTA'S FINAL STOP. A decades-long tradition ended in November of 1982, when Santa accepted the key to the city in front of his magic castle on Hudson's Woodward marquee for the last time. A store closing clearance began shortly after the 1982 holiday season. (Courtesy of Douglas Peters.)

OUTSIDE ENTRANCE ONE. The lucrative location outside Entrance One on Woodward was utilized through the years by vendors selling popcorn, peanuts, and roasted chestnuts. The holidays also brought out the cheerful bell ringers from the Salvation Army as well as the occasional chants of members of the Hare Krishna. (Courtesy of Douglas Peters.)

ELEVATORS AS FAR AS THE EYE COULD SEE. The massive bank of elevators in the Second Floor Men's Department was especially impressive. The stately mahogany walls along with the brass drinking fountains provided an elegant feel. This floor also featured large French windows on the Woodward side. (Courtesy of Douglas Peters.)

STAIRWAYS. There were five principal stair routes in the store. Each staircase was adorned with cast-iron railings and polished mahogany handrails. The Grand River stairwell was blessed with natural light as its route was adjacent to windows from the Mezzanine to the 15th Floor. (Courtesy of Douglas Peters.)

BRASS DRINKING FOUNTAINS. Ask anyone what they remember about the downtown store and invariably they will mention the beautiful brass drinking fountains which graced many selling floors of the store. The Fourth Floor fountains were scaled shorter for children. An original fountain was restored and can be viewed on the main floor of Somerset Marshall Field's. (Courtesy of Douglas Peters.)

THE *HUDSONIAN* CELEBRATES MEMORIES. The Holiday 1982 edition of the *Hudsonian*, Hudson's employee magazine, was devoted to memories of the downtown store. This in-house magazine was founded in 1913 and was one of the oldest employee publications in the retail industry. (Courtesy of Michael Hauser.)

108

THE J. L. HUDSON COMPANY

DETROIT, MICHIGAN 48226

P. GERALD MILLS
CHAIRMAN AND
CHIEF EXECUTIVE OFFICER

Dear Hudsonian:

After years of study and deliberation we are announcing today a most difficult decision for The J. L. Hudson Company. The Downtown Store operation will close following the 1982 holiday season.

This announcement has great impact on all of us. Yet, the employees most affected are the Hudsonians in the Downtown Store who undoubtedly have anxiety over the future of their jobs. I want to emphasize that all Downtown Store Hudson's employees will be offered positions at another metro store. I want also to emphasize that no Hudson's employees at other stores will lose their jobs as a result of this closing.

Many considerations played a part in the decision to discontinue this retail operation, but the well being of all Hudson's employees was a constant concern. Particularly in the current economic environment, we are pleased to be able to offer all downtown Hudson's employees opportunities for further employment.

Now let me share with you why this closing decision was made.

As many of you can recall, talk of closing the Downtown Store has been circulating throughout the Company and Detroit community for years. The primary reason for this was the long-term downtrend of sales in the Downtown Store. This trend can be traced back 20 years and was consistent in its downward pattern even during Detroit's more prosperous years. We did everything in our power to turn that trend around, but the fact is that our Downtown Store continues to operate at a loss.

Over the last five years, Hudson's has worked with City and community leaders on the proposed Cadillac Mall project. From the very beginning of that project, Hudson's made it clear that the only way we would participate in the proposed mall was with other major retailers. In the course of all this time, no other major retailer has made a commitment to this project. Despite all the best efforts of the Mayor, the City administration, the Federal Government, and other community leaders, there appears little hope for the project's implementation in the foreseeable future.

Last year we implemented programs in the Downtown store designed to improve business. We remodeled selling areas, improved the merchandise mix and expanded special events to build customer traffic. In spite of all these efforts, the hard fact remains that the Downtown Store sales continued to deteriorate throughout 1981 and 1982.

Our studies indicate that consumers have changed their shopping patterns in recent decades. They prefer a shopping environment that contains several major stores, a variety of specialty shops, easy access from their homes, and nearby free parking.

Hudson's is the last major retailer in downtown Detroit, as we have been for the last several years. The size of the building, over two million square feet, makes it an expensive and inefficient arena to do business in.

All of these factors have contributed significantly to present and forecasted operating losses for the Downtown Store. As a result,

the Company's ongoing financial support of the Downtown Store can no longer be justified. The decision at this point in time is in favor of the overall well being of Hudson's as a Company. Hudson's is today a healthy company, and we intend to stay that way.

Although the Downtown Store operations will close after the holidays, Hudson's Corporate Offices will remain in the downtown building. There are no plans for relocation of these offices in the short term. We will be conducting studies to determine the best facility for eventual relocation.

As a result of this announcement, I am sure that many of you will have unanswered questions. To support this need, our personnel staff will be available through the Open Line phone number (3-1106) beginning today. Your questions are encouraged. They will be answered in the quickest and best way possible.

The tradition of Hudson's as a premier retailer is one we want to preserve. In the remaining months that the Downtown Store is open, we will continue to offer our customers quality merchandise and service.

As always, your professionalism and support are essential and would be greatly appreciated. Working together as a team, we will close our Downtown Store with the dignity and grace it deserves.

P. Gerald Mills

July 14, 1982

THE DREADED ANNOUNCEMENT. Downtown store employees received this letter on July 14, 1982. The next day, it was front page news in both Detroit dailies. Virtually every major newspaper in the country ran a story, including *The New York Times*. Countless editorials and stories followed the initial announcement. (Courtesy of Michael Hauser.)

A DECADE LATER, TEMPORARY ADAPTIVE RE-USE. For the 1992 holiday season, under different ownership, the Main Floor of Hudson's re-opened as a "Gift Mart." Large generators were brought in to light up the selling floor and produce heat for guests. The purpose was to draw public awareness, in the hope of securing a developer. (Courtesy of Michael Hauser.)

THE LIGHTS FLICKER BRIEFLY. The 1992 "Gift Mart" lasted between Thanksgiving and Christmas. It drew some curiosity seekers, but was only marginally successful. The event marked the final time that the public would be allowed to legally enter the building. (Courtesy of Michael Hauser.)

Eight

CREATING A LASTING MEMORY

ROOFTOP VISIT. In 1993, Preservation Wayne, metro Detroit's oldest and largest non-profit historic preservation group, was contacted by one of the owners of the Hudson's building to create window scenes with other non-profits in an attempt to spruce up the property. Volunteers were locked in the store for an entire day to determine which items could be salvaged for display purposes. Pictured are Preservation Wayne members on the 25th Floor roof, from left to right: Jeff Garland, Brian Hurttienne, Victor Maggio, author Michael Hauser, James Luzenski, Rebecca Savage, and Kyle Viger. (Courtesy of Jeff Garland.)

A 20TH-CENTURY ARCHEOLOGICAL EXPEDITION. In September of 1996, Preservation Wayne volunteers began photographically documenting Hudson's for the Greater Downtown Partnership. Meanwhile, the Partnership was also in discussion with the Detroit Historical Museum to produce an exhibit on the store as a way to present a positive "final closure" for the public prior to demolition. Above is a mahogany panel salvaged from the Second Floor. (Courtesy of Michael Hauser.)

HIDDEN SODA FOUNTAIN TILES. In November of 1996, the Detroit Historical Museum appointed Michael Hauser as guest curator for the "Remembering Downtown Hudson's" exhibit. Hauser and the Preservation Wayne volunteers worked each weekend in the darkened store for almost a year, retrieving items for the exhibit and documenting all 32 levels of the store with photographs. The above image depicts hand-painted ceramic tiles in the Soda Fountain that were covered over in a 1950s remodeling. (Courtesy of Michael Hauser.)

HIDDEN PLASTER DETAIL. Plaster ornamentation such as that depicted at right on the Ninth Floor could be found in many walled-off areas of the store. The volunteers would collect and package items for the exhibit, and at the end of the day, carry all objects to the Main Floor Dock. Much of this work had to be done with high-powered flashlights as there was no electricity. (Courtesy of Michael Hauser.)

MECHANICAL WONDERS IN THE THIRD BASEMENT. One afternoon in the darkest corner of the Third Basement, the researchers discovered this Detroit Edison "trigger board," which distributed steam to all levels of the store. Detroit Edison additionally had three electrical substations in the building. (Courtesy of Michael Hauser.)

REMNANTS OF THE TUBE ROOM. Much of the Tube Room with its ornamental "triggers" had been vandalized. Amazingly, there were no carriers to be found anywhere. A portion of the conveyor belt was still intact, as were the large blowers that powered this amazing system. (Courtesy of Kevin Piotrowski.)

FOLLOWING A HARD DAY ON THE JOB. This image depicts one of three foot tubs, each located in private rooms in the 14th Floor Hospital. This is where sales associates could rest their feet in comfort after a long day on the selling floor. Initially, many of the selling floors were wood, prior to the installation of carpeting. (Courtesy of Michael Hauser.)

A DIFFERENT TYPE OF PENTHOUSE.
Long after the store closed, a guard with "man's best friend" would thoroughly check each floor for intruders or "sleepovers." Hudson's Bouvier watchdog had quarters on the 15th Floor roof of the Farmer Building. Amazingly, the dog house was still there in 1997. (Courtesy of Michael Hauser.)

LET'S TAKE THE "CROSSOVER"!
Children loved to whoosh through the revolving doors and cross the covered alley that connected the South Woodward and Farmer Buildings. "Watch for trucks" was emblazoned above each entrance, as this was a "live" passageway for delivery trucks heading to and from the store delivery dock. (Courtesy of Michael Hauser.)

ICE FORMATIONS IN APRIL! The lower depths of the store in 1997 could not distinguish seasons. These large ice formations were common sights in the Third Basement, due to damaged drain pipes and water streaming down elevator shafts. On many cold days, volunteer researchers' cameras and food supply would freeze up. (Courtesy of Michael Hauser.)

WATER, WATER EVERYWHERE. In the spring of 1997, contractors spent several months pumping water out of the Fourth Basement, which was completely engulfed with water from a burst city waterline. A limited number of gallons per day were allowed into the sewer system. The image below was taken outside of the Building Superintendent's Office. (Courtesy of Michael Hauser.)

LAYERING UP WHILE SCOUTING FOR EXHIBIT ITEMS. Even with barrel fires set up by contractors removing various equipment from the Third Basement, the temperatures were numbing. Volunteer Rebecca Savage, shown here amongst some of the heating and cooling apparatus, is dressed several layers thick to stay somewhat warm. (Courtesy of Michael Hauser.)

HIDDEN TREASURE IN UNLIKELY PLACES. Some of the most interesting "finds" for the museum exhibit were the most difficult to retrieve. At left, volunteers Dan Kosmowski, Kyle Viger, and Lance Myers remove layers of particle board that concealed an intact mahogany and glass store directory from 1948. Other fascinating objects found for the exhibit included elevator signs and call signals, store log books from the 1940s, and numerous employee name badges and uniforms. (Courtesy of Michael Hauser.)

117

LAST BUFFET IN THE PINE ROOM. Despite several years of scavengers removing or destroying anything of value, the Pine Room survived relatively intact. Due to the amount of territory covered by the volunteers in a given day with no electricity, bottled water and granola bars were the most efficient way to combat thirst and hunger. Preservation Wayne researchers would agree to meet for these meals in the Pine Room at a designated time. (Courtesy of Lance Myers.)

PHOTODOCUMENTING EVERY SQUARE INCH! Preservation Wayne volunteers Laszlo Regos and Lance Myers prepare to photograph the 17th Floor Fur Vaults. The crew shot several thousand images throughout the 32-level Hudson's Building. Color and black and white images as well as slides were provided to the Greater Downtown Partnership and the National Building Museum. (Courtesy of Michael Hauser.)

PENTHOUSE WONDERS. In this image, Preservation Wayne volunteer Maura Cady is dwarfed by one of the three 45,000-gallon fire suppression water tanks on the 25th Floor. One elevator serviced the tower to the 24th Floor. From there, one walked up a dark staircase to 25, passing the catwalk on the exterior of the building where the nine-foot letters spelling out HUDSON'S were formerly affixed. (Courtesy of Michael Hauser.)

ON TOP OF THE WORLD! This image depicts the enormous height of the 25th Floor. Preservation Wayne volunteer Kyle Viger is barely visible. Visual Merchandising occasionally utilized this as a staging area. In 1957, murals for Hudson's Eastland store were painted in this area. (Courtesy of Michael Hauser.)

LITTLE-KNOWN EXTERIOR DETAILS. Much of the exterior ornamentation of Hudson's was not visible to passersby. This image captures some of the ornate terra cotta cornice and Romanesque arches, as seen from the 16th Floor on the Woodward side. (Courtesy of Michael Hauser.)

HIGH ABOVE WOODWARD. This is a view from the 17th Floor adjacent to the Fur Vaults. The upper floors of Hudson's featured a series of set backs. The overall structure suggested a combination of Beaux Arts terra cotta ornamentation combined with classic Chicago-style façade treatment. (Courtesy of Michael Hauser.)

THE TOWERING GIANT. This 1996 image illustrates the might of the Hudson's Building, which was literally an engineering marvel. The Downtown Library in the foreground is engulfed by the massiveness of the store, which covered the entire area of its 220-by-420-foot city block. (Courtesy of Michael Hauser.)

DETAILED CORNICES. The Grand River and Tower additions to the store feature historically-derived style treatments such as Renaissance-inspired pediment windows, banded Norman arches, and a Baroque shell motif. The 15th Floor was capped with an ornate denticular cornice. (Courtesy of Michael Hauser.)

MORE UNIQUE TERRA COTTA. Just outside the 12th Floor Auditorium, these Baroque shell motifs of glazed terra cotta stood guard over busy Woodward Avenue. This expanse of detail was complemented with copper flashing. Periodically, portions of this façade appear on eBay for $800 per shell. (Courtesy of Michael Hauser.)

LOOKING UP AT THE GREAT HUDSON TOWER. Unless you were a curious employee, few folks were able to view this portion of the tower from the 20th Floor roof, looking upwards. Architecturally, the tower appears to have been treated as a separate structure and invokes strong Art Deco features. Non-selling functions such as laundry, sign shop, elevator maintenance, and an executive workout area were located on these floors. (Courtesy of Jeff Garland.)

1891	An eight-story full-line store was constructed at Gratiot Avenue and Farmer Street. The architect was Mortimer L. Smith. At the time, Hudson's was the second tallest structure in Detroit.
1907	An eight-story addition opened just north of the original "big store."
1911	The original 1891/1907 complex was given a 12-story addition, providing Hudson's with its first frontage on Woodward Avenue. This section was actually built in seven separately matched sections between 1911 and 1919. Smith, Hinchman and Grylls were the architects.
1923	The 1891 and 1907 buildings were demolished to make way for the 1925 addition.
1925	A 15-story addition at Farmer and Gratiot was completed. Smith, Hinchman and Grylls were the architects.
1925	Two additional floors (11th and 12th) were added to the Woodward Avenue frontage. Smith, Hinchman and Grylls were the architects.
1927	J.L. Hudson Co. purchased the Newcomb Endicott Department Store. Newcomb's structures at Woodward and Grand River Avenues were demolished and replaced with a 16-story addition, with a portion that extended into a 25-story tower. This L-shaped addition was built in two separate matched segments between 1925 and 1928. Smith, Hinchman and Grylls were the architects. (The 17th and 18th Floors were added to the Grand River/Woodward building in 1928.)
1928	"The Big Store" became "The Greater Hudson Store" encompassing almost an entire city block.
1946	A final 12-story addition was constructed at Woodward and Gratiot, site of the former Sallan Building. This was the final parcel on the block. Smith, Hinchman and Grylls were the architects.
1946	Two additional floors (19th and 20th) were added to the Grand River end of the building. The Mezzanine was also expanded. Smith, Hinchman and Grylls were the architects.
1946	Hudson's now contained 2.2 million square feet, 49 acres of floor space and 12,000 employees in this building

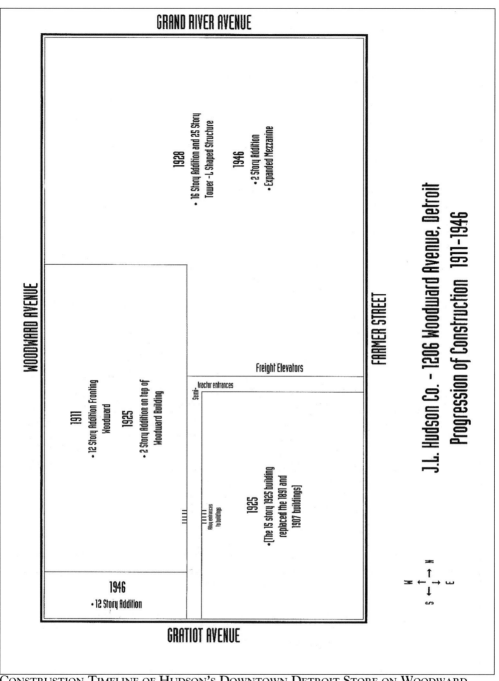

CONSTRUSTION TIMELINE OF HUDSON'S DOWNTOWN DETROIT STORE ON WOODWARD AVENUE. (Courtesy of Glenda Smith.)

1983	In January, the retail operation at 1206 Woodward Avenue closed its doors after 92 years of operating at this location. The corporate offices for all Hudson's stores remained on various floors of the downtown building employing 1,200 associates.
1984	The retail operations of Dayton's (Minneapolis) and Hudson's (Detroit) merge. Corporate headquarters begins a gradual move to Minneapolis (including buying offices, advertising, public relations, executive offices, and many non-selling centers).
1985	Adjusted employment at corporate headquarters is pared down to 250 associates.
1986	Towards the end of the year, credit operations, the final corporate department in the building, made the move to Minneapolis. Approximately 50 associates moved to the new Region One headquarters at Northland Center.
1987	Hudson's maintains a skeleton staff of maintenance/operations associates in the building. The structure still has electricity, heat, water, elevator service, and security.
1989 1990	Hudson's sells their landmark building to Southwestern Associates of Windsor, Ontario. In January, Hudson's removes all brass nameplates from the exterior of the building. Helicopters arrived to remove the nine-foot-high copper clad "HUDSON'S" letters from all four sides of the tower. By spring of 1990, it became apparent that the new owners did not have the ability to fund and implement a renovation of the building. The City of Detroit became concerned when the new owners shut off electricity and illegally disconnected the fire suppression system. City inspectors discovered that the building was being stripped of copper, brass, and nickel. Additionally, elevators and escalators were also being gutted.
1992	Ownership of the building was still murky. Several parties claimed ownership rights. To interest developers, a "Gift Mart" operated on the Main Floor between Thanksgiving and Christmas, which was administered by a local developer and architect who claimed partial ownership.
1994- 1995	This period of time is when the building became most vulnerable to outside organized scrap dealers. Several parties actually took up residence in the building and made a profession of pilfering each floor at a time. Several fires resulted from these illegal activities.
1996	The Greater Downtown Partnership was created by Mayor Archer to propose solutions for the Hudson block and gain control of the property. Both a developer and a church claimed ownership at this point, despite the fact no one was paying taxes on the property or providing security. In mid-1996, the Partnership gained title to the property. They contacted Preservation Wayne to photodocument the structure. After much discussion with community leaders, the Archer administration felt the only positive solution for the future of the Hudson block was to demolish the property. Larry Marantette of the Partnership, and Maud Lyon, then director of the Detroit Historical Museum, felt that a positive way to bring closure to the demolition would be to stage an exhibit on Hudson's at the museum. Michael Hauser was selected to be guest curator for the "Remembering Downtown Hudson's" exhibit at the Detroit Historical Museum. He amassed a dedicated contingent of volunteers from Preservation Wayne who photodocumented and toiled for exhibit objects in the vacant 2.2 million-square-foot structure. This 20th century archeological hunt spanned almost a year, with the exhibit opening in August of 1997.
1997	Contractors begin to demolish sections of the vast Hudson complex, preparing the structure for the implosion.
1998	On October 24, 1998 at 5:45 p.m. (store closing time) Hudson's became the largest structure ever to be imploded.

Opposite: **TIMELINE OF EVENTS FOLLOWING THE CLOSURE OF HUDSON'S DOWNTOWN DETROIT STORE.** Note: Contrary to consistent misinformation from the media, the Hudson's Building had not been vacant for 14 years, but realistically, for seven years.

THE LIGHTS GO OUT FOR GOOD. In January of 1990, helicopters removed the last visible sign of Detroit's world famous department store. The HUDSON'S letters on all four sides of the tower were an area landmark since 1928. (New letters replaced the original ones in 1950.) The letters were copper with heavy white porcelain enamel. More than 1,300 feet of neon tubing was utilized to light the signage. Each letter was 9 feet tall. (Courtesy Target Corporation Archives.)

The Hudson Creed

I believe in Hudson's because into its make-up have gone the finest thoughts of those at its head.

I believe in Hudson's because I am putting into it myself — the best that is in me.

I believe in Hudson's because, back of every piece of merchandise which crosses the counter, there is something which says to the customer: "If not satisfactory, this may be returned and full value given therefor"; furthermore, each and every piece of merchandise is the best that can be produced at the price.

My faith is not alone a faith in the store, the organization — it's a faith in the ideals of men, those who are responsible for this great house of industry.

And so I stand, inspired with the blazing truth that I am taking an active part in building, through honest effort, one of the greatest institutions in this broad country — Hudson's, Detroit.

THE HUDSON CREED. This was written by Mr. Hudson as a standard for all of his future employees. It appeared in all employee manuals, work rooms, rest areas, and service halls. (Courtesy of Target Corporation Archives.)